W9-BXX-147

Howlin' at the Dixie Moon

A Collection of Columns
About Life in the Blessed South

By Don Lively

Otter Bay Books
BALTIMORE, MARYLAND 2010

Copyright © 2010 by
Don Lively
All rights reserved.

Permission to reproduce in any form
must be secured from the author.

Please direct all correspondence and book orders to:
Don Lively
515 Seven Oaks Road
Waynesboro, GA 30830

email: livelycolo@aol.com

Library of Congress Control Number 2010936888
ISBN 978-0-615-40799-9

Published for the author by
Otter Bay Books, LLC
3507 Newland Road
Baltimore, MD 21218-2513

Printed in the United States of America

Dedication

To Mama and Daddy
who raised me right in spite of myself
before they flew off to Heaven.

To the three young humans
who I helped bring into the world,
and to the two (so far) grands,
all of whom have their fair share
of Southern genetics
coursing through them.

To Mrs. Tinley, who left Earth way to soon,
who convinced me that I could write,
and to Strick, my college journalism advisor,
who helped me polish up my wordsmithery.

To the one who got away
but the memory of whose enchanting eyes
even now, all these years later,
makes me want to be a good man.

To Dixie, my homeland.

TABLE of CONTENTS

PREFACE

Very seldom does a week pass without somebody telling me that my column is the first thing that they turn to when the paper comes out. I've often been encouraged to compile some of my best ones into a book.

Well, here you go.

Writing about life in the South is easy really, though you might not believe that if you saw me sitting staring bleary-eyed at my word processor on some Sunday nights, not having written a sentence or even come up with a decent idea as to what story to tell with my allotted eight hundred words that are due at noon on Monday. But generally, the South itself gives a writer plenty of ammo to fight off the occasional writer's block.

If you're Southern, or from any place in rural America, you'll recognize yourself or somebody you know in these pages. You may not have known my Uncle Cuz, but there's somebody in your family who blesses you with his overshadowing patriarchal guidance. You might not have ever heard of Danny's Dairy Bar but there was some similar place in the past of your young years where you and your friends hung out. You were probably never sprayed point blank by a skunk in his last defiant act, or chased out of a cypress swamp by a flaming ghost but I'm sure you've had your own misadventures.

As long as there's a place called Dixie, as long as there are dirt roads and peculiar kinfolk and peanut patches and a vast array of folks who proudly call themselves Southerners, there will be plenty to write about.

You'll have to judge if these are indeed some of my best. I just know they're some of my favorites.

ACKNOWLEDGMENTS

A whole bunch of folks deserve a big ol' rowdy Southern "thank you kindly" for helping make this dream of mine come true. Putting a book together is a lot bigger project than I ever imagined. Lots of people made it possible.

My sincere thanks to Roy for giving me the opportunity to write for the True Citizen, and to Bonnie, who I've known since we were kids, for saving me space every week to do my scribbling.

To CCT who reads almost everything I write before it's published and who has, so far, never read anything she didn't like, thanks lady.

To my huge, eccentric, loud and proud family, for giving me an endless supply of stories to tell, many thanks. I wouldn't trade our clan for any other.

To all of you who have emailed or called or snail mailed or come up to me at church or in a store or a restaurant to tell me how much you enjoy my columns, I can't begin to tell you how much I appreciate you reading me. You make it fun. Thank you.

To my two Yankee friends who were also my partners for over twenty years on the streets. Donn, who I call Typo, since nobody would intentionally spell it that way on a birth certificate, thank you for the input from a "less than Southern" perspective. And Dawn, for all those 4am meets where I "tried out" so many of the stories that eventually made it into my writing, thanks for staying awake (most of the time).

Ann at Otter Bay Books and Kate at Heron and Earth Design have been invaluable in their expertise and abundantly patient in dealing with me, the neophyte author. Thank you ladies.

And finally, to the people of the Blessed South, and really to folks all over rural America, thank you for the perpetual inspiration.

From way down South in Dixie, thank yall.

I

THE YOUNG YEARS

"When I was younger I could remember anything,
whether it happened or not."

~ Mark Twain ~

Losing Them |

Dixie dirt farmers, that's what we were.

I employ the term with the utmost affection.

I had to admit at a very young age that I was not cut out to be a full time farmer, but, I wouldn't swap the farm years for forty fortunes.

You can love something even if you don't have an aptitude for it.

I enjoy playing golf but my total for a typical eighteen holes normally resembles an NBA basketball score. Both teams combined score some days.

I like to dance but the last time I did somebody called the paramedics cause they thought I was having a seizure.

I liked being married but, well, I'm not. Let's just leave it at that.

So, even though my farming fortunes ended as soon as Daddy was able to pack me off to college, it was great fun growing up in the country.

On the dirt farm.

Actually, there was a time when he also had livestock.

To me, that was the best part of farming.

The animals.

We kept a few cows, a few pigs, a yard full of chickens and a goat or two.

One of my jobs was to go to the barn just after dark and throw a hundred ears of dry corn to the cows. I loved watching them eat and listening to them crunch their meal.

One year Daddy bought a milk cow. He decided he didn't like paying eighty-nine cents a gallon when we could get fresh milk from our own cow for much less.

Seemed logical.

Except he wasn't successful teaching any of us how to milk the old girl and what little milk he did get from her none of us would drink.

So, we took her back to the stock yard.

Our main livestock venture was pigs.

Daddy bought a few sows and a couple of mean old bo-hogs. That combination produced dozens of squealing little pigs a few months later.

I liked feeding them. Filling up the water troughs and wallows from the hose pipe. Occasionally scratching them behind the ears.

They were as cute as speckled puppies.

I liked the baby pigs.

For a while.

Until yet another traumatic event happened in my young life.

One morning, just after breakfast, Daddy told my brothers and me that we had a job to do at the pig parlor.

That was fine with me. Anything to do with the pigs beat weed pulling or stump toting.

Or so I thought.

I knew the pigs had already been fed so I wondered what job needed doing.

" What are we going to do Daddy?"

" We're going to castrate the pigs."

I had no idea what that meant, but, not wanting to appear ignorant, I pulled Urb aside and asked him if he understood.

He did.

He described the process in vivid detail.

I freaked.

" We're going to cut their WHATS off?"

" We're going to make gentlemen out of them," Daddy

chuckled.

It was years before I actually got the joke.

Removing those vital parts eliminated their ability to act in an ungentlemanly manner toward the lady pigs.

Daddy saw that I was panicking so he tried to reassure me.

" They won't feel a thing."

I remember thinking, " I'd sure as the devil feel it if it happened to me!"

I'd taken hits "down there" playing football on a few occasions. It hurts!

To actually cut them out with a razor!

That was nuts!

So to speak.

But, I was a farm boy and I had no choice but to pitch in.

It was nasty work.

The animals were squealing and kicking like they knew they were about to become eunuchs.

I was getting through it okay though, squeezing, slitting, tugging, throwing the parts into a bucket.

Then it happened.

I must have been a little too close to the blade cause when the cut was made the disgusting juices squirted out like a firehose.

Straight into my eyes.

I squealed like one of the victim piglets.

I was done!

I didn't care what Daddy whupped me with, I wasn't going to disconnect one more innocent little critter from his mountain oysters.

I headed for the water spigot, turned the handle and doused my eyes for the rest of the morning.

" *They won't feel a thing.*"

Yeah, right.

At the very least the whole episode hurt their pride and dignity. And ended their chances settle down with a nice little girl pig.

Thankfully, it turned out that pig pee is not a blinding agent, so my eyesight survived the ordeal.

That was my first, and last, foray into animal husbandry and even though I understand how the practice is important to pork production, I'd just as soon leave that job to somebody else.

A few years later Daddy decided to go strictly dirt farm. Pretty soon all the animals were gone.

I missed them. The cows. The chickens. The goats.

And, except for the day that all the males learned to sing tenor, I even missed the pigs, though not as much as I'm sure they missed their family jewels.

Not nearly.

Boys And Summer |

Sultry days like we experience around our neck of the woods pretty much all summer sometimes makes me question the wisdom of leaving the milder climes of the Rocky Mountain West to move back South.

Denver was actually built on what is known geologically as a high desert, at least that's what I've been told by folks who possess more knowledge than I have in that area. So it does get hot there. Hot but not humid. You could make the short drive into the foothills and find cool air. Drive high enough and you would find snow fields easily accessible all summer long.

You could escape the heat.

Not where I live now, in the humidity capitol of the world.

You know all about humidity if you've lived in the South long. It's that weather phenomenon that causes your shirt to stick to your skin the second you walk outside during the summer.

It's also the reason that I occasionally long to head westbound until I see aspen trees.

I sometimes question exactly who created humidity. I suspect that it arrived from the nether regions along with fire ants but I'll leave that to the theologians and meteorologists to ponder.

My family has had a way to beat the heat for nearly a century. An oasis from those oppressive waves of steamy airborne moisture.

The Pond.

It's much more than a swimming hole.

The Pond is nearly sacred to my kinfolk. The Pond refers to the whole tract of land but the best part in the middle of the summer IS the swimming hole.

It's fed by several underground springs and the water is so cold that it's not advisable to try to ease into it. It's best to just hold your breath and jump. You hold your breath because if you don't the frigid water will snatch it out of your lungs.

Over the years hundreds of folks have frolicked in the clear pool with the white sand bottom.

One summer several of my town friends were visiting me. We were too young to drive so we rode our bicycles from the house to The Pond. The group consisted of myself, Mike, Wheatie, David and my cousin Michael. Michael wasn't from town, he lived right down the road from me, but he had recently moved South from up north so he might as well have been.

The ride was short but it was a hot day and by the time we arrived the cold green water looked very inviting.

There was only one problem. We hadn't brought swimming suits. Wheatie suggested that we go skinny dipping but none of us were that proud of our fifteen year old bodies so we settled for stripping down to our drawers.

Except for Wheatie. Seems he hadn't troubled himself with underwear that day so he went into The Pond commando style.

We had a cable and pulley stretched over The Pond that we could hang onto and ride down the wire into the water. Wheatie decided to try it buck naked.

Wheatie was easily the skinniest of all my friends. A hundred pounds soaking wet. So when he leapt from the tree holding onto the pulley, his weight wasn't enough to move the contraption very far. It stopped, stranding him, in all his glory, 15 feet over the water. To make matters worse, his fingers got caught in the rope and he couldn't let go and drop into the pond.

About that time is when my aunt showed up. The rest of us, in our own near state of undress, hid as much as we could under the water. My aunt parked her car and walked down the hill to the pond. She spotted Wheatie hanging there. He only had the use of one hand and was trying frantically but unsuccessfully to utilize it to maintain his dignity and conceal as much as he possibly could.

"Are you stuck up there?' my aunt asked.

"Yes ma'am", Wheatie weakly replied.

She then turned her attention to the other four heads sticking out of the water.

" Do yall intend to leave him there or should I call the fire department?"

"No!" Wheatie screamed, not as weakly, no doubt imagining the story spreading like wildfire.

" We'll get him down when you leave", I volunteered.

We could hear her laughing as she drove away.

We were finally able to get Wheatie down though it was quite unpleasant having one underwear clad boy standing on my shoulders trying to free unclad Wheatie. When he did come loose both of them fell directly on top of me.

It must have been quite a sight.

To this day, that aunt has never mentioned the incident.

I'm guessing that Wheatie never has either.

Old School Days |

The two old brick buildings are at the center of a controversy over what to do with them, tear them down, renovate them, or ignore them and hope they disappear, but to me they represent a huge part of my past.

My elementary and junior high schools, still looking dignified years later.

Driving by the buildings I remember on the first day of school laying eyes on folks for the first time who I am still friends with today. It's where my life away from the farm began. Where the world became much bigger.

Seeing the old structures brings back a flood of memories.

I remember that Mama bought me a couple of fat red pencils with no erasers and a Blue Horse writing tablet with lined sheets of paper inside. They were tucked into a brand new book satchel with my other school supplies. I could not have been prouder if I'd been carrying the Holy Grail itself.

All of the desks, no doubt old surplus items, had little round holes in the upper right hand corner. The holes were inkwells where little jars of the black writing fluid were placed for the old style pens to be dipped. Always in the upper right corner. I sometimes wondered why there were no left handed holes. The inkwells had long since gone out of use by the time I started school.

The classrooms always smelled like turpentine. The floors were wood with no rugs or carpet and were always slick and shiny. There were no reading rooms and media centers like there are in modern schools. Your day was spent in your desk facing forward.

The walls at the front of the classrooms were covered with green chalkboards. The chalk was white. After several days of wiping written instructions from the boards the chalk erasers would require cleaning. It was quite an honor to be designated by the teacher to "dust the erasers". She would send the appointed student out to the playground where there was an old tree stump that seemed to serve only one purpose, having the erasers beaten against it until all the chalk dust was on the stump and off of the erasers.

Then, as now, the kids favorite part of school was not school at all.

It was recess.

Recess meant playtime. The playground was covered with several different pieces of equipment designed to keep the students active and busy during recess.

Monkey bars. Jungle gyms. And my favorite, the Giant Strides.

It was a tall metal pole with eight chains attached to a rotating wheel at the top. At the end of each chain was a handle grip where a kid could hold on. The eight participants would run around in a circle holding onto the chains until everybody became nearly airborne. You could "fly" twenty feet or so without your shoes touching the ground. Every now and then someone would lose their grip and go flying off into the dirt tearing the knees out of their pants and scraping off a couple of layers of skin.

It was great fun but somewhere along the line somebody decided it was much too dangerous so the Giant Strides were removed along with the other apparatus.

Drive by some schools today and all you see on the playground is...ground.

These days push pins hold posters and other paper documents in place on the corkboards but back then there were thumbtacks. I feel certain that within five minutes of the first box of thumbtacks being introduced to academia, some imaginative pupil decided what fun it would be to put one pointing up in somebody's desk for that person to sit on. It's a prank that has played itself out thousands of times always with the same result. The victim would plop down on the hard seat only to have his behind pierced by the tack causing him to yelp and jump up out of the desk resulting in total disruption to the rest of the class. The teacher would try in vain to get somebody to confess to the crime. It never happened.

The end of the school day meant boarding the bus and heading home. In those days there was a tradition known as "running the tracks". When the bus would arrive at a railroad crossing a kid would be selected by the driver to get off and cross the tracks ahead of the bus, presumably to warn against approaching locomotives. I don't remember any close calls but for some reason the practice was stopped years ago.

Running the tracks. Dusting the erasers. Thumbtacks. Giant Strides. Gone. Faded into history.

I hope the same fate doesn't await the two fine old buildings.

THE BEST BAD HABITS |

Bad habits are hard to break.

That's why January 1st was invented, so people could make halfhearted pledges to alter old behaviors.

Out with the bad habits, in with the good.

Yea right.

I've only found one thing harder to do than breaking the old habits.

Starting them.

Cultivating frowned upon inclinations is hard work.

Let me explain.

My first bad habit, and probably the easiest to begin, was cussing. I don't actually remember the first time I cussed but I do remember the guilt I felt when a vile word first escaped my lips. I'd heard the words but hadn't used them for fear of going to the bad place where the booger man lived. The words "hell" and "devil" were not permissible even though both are graphically described and thoroughly documented in the Bible.

I discussed cussing with Daddy when I was about seven.

"What's so bad about cussin? I love to cuss and sometimes there ain't nothin' else to say", I said, stating my case.

" Well, every time you feel like cussin' just holler BILLY GOAT", Daddy replied, offering me an alternate epitaph while no doubt stifling a chuckle.

I tried it. It worked for a while. Until I said it at school in front of my new city friends and was roundly ridiculed.

Actually, I do still utilize Billy Goat every now and then if a mild expletive is required.

Somewhere along the way I decided that I wanted to smoke. I read western novels when I was young and all of the cowboys, good guys and black hats alike, smoked. One of my heroes smoked Bull Durhams. That sounded tough. That would be my brand. I was too smart to try to buy cigarettes from Mister Scott at the store across the road so one day while visiting with a buddy in town we went to a little store and I asked for Bull Durhams only to learn that those were the "roll your own" type.

The store owner, obviously unconcerned about selling tobacco to a ten year old, recommended something called Raleighs. We left the store and headed straight for the woods where we lit up and prepared to look very cool.

I'd never tasted anything so nasty in my life. Still haven't. I turned forty shades of green but I managed to smoke about half of the pack before getting so light headed that I had to lay in the weeds for an hour.

I chewed some green pine needles to mask the smell but must have still stunk to high Paradise cause Mama later asked me which of my friend's parents was a smoker.

"Both of them", I lied. Another bad habit.

My first taste of alcohol was memorable.

I was bringing a tractor in from the field when I saw our farm hand standing with his friends by the road. He flagged me over and handed me a Mason jar filled with clear liquid. He encouraged me to take a swallow and, not wanting to be a sissy, I chugged it.

I didn't feel it right away, in fact I didn't feel anything except paralysis. Then without warning my throat felt like there was a wildcat trying to claw it's way into my innards.

It was moonshine.

White lightening.

He called it scrap iron.

I hurried off so that they wouldn't see me when that wildcat reversed course and came back up.

My first chew took place on a school bus riding home from a road game. I was a freshman and my cousin Wrong Way, a senior, handed me his Red Man. I acceded.

He forgot to tell me to spit, not swallow. Minutes later I was bent over with my face buried in a paper Piggly Wiggly bag sick as a mule on sour hay. I was on the outside of the seat with poor Henry trapped on the inside. I can still see the look of terror on his face.

We both survived the ordeal and, even though I was humiliated and disoriented for a week, I still took up chewing in later years.

How intelligent are humans to start habits where the foremost requirement is to avoid vomiting?

Those first smokes made me choke, then gag, and caused me to have to fib to Mama, yet I started smoking anyway.

The illegally distilled white liquor nearly debilitated me. I started partaking just the same.

Even though I have quit or greatly curtailed most of those old habits, it wasn't easy.

But getting started was even harder.

Harder than "Billy Goat".

Going To The Fair |

Recently, when the fair was in town, it reminded me of one of the most traumatic days of my young life.

The day Daddy took us to the Richmond County Fair.

I'd been to the fair in our little town many times, but this trip promised to be much more exciting!

We'd all looked forward to it for days. When we got there I thought that it had to be the biggest fairgrounds on Earth. It must have been ten times the size of our fair.

I was in awe.

There were so many rides that I'd never seen. Dozens of games to be tried, most often to be lost, but nonetheless captivating for a young farm boy. There were also what were called back then "freak shows" politically incorrect language today, but that's how they were billed. I know now that they were mostly fake but back then I was fascinated by the Turtle Woman and the Three Legged Man. They looked real to my ten year old eyes!

I ran into a school buddy while I was walking around gawking. We passed by the "hoochie coochie" tent and the man standing outside was announcing the arrival of Falana, the exotic dancer from Egypt. Before we could object the guy just grabbed a quarter from each of us and shoved us through the flaps. All these years later I remember what Falana looked like and I remember thinking that she didn't look Egyptian to me. She looked like any other American. In fact, if she hadn't been wearing such thick makeup I'd have sworn she worked with Mama at the Piggly Wiggly. But, at that point I didn't really care what her national origins were, I was more focused on what she was able to do with the two tassels attached to two strategic parts of her costume. I was nearly hypnotized but at one point I did glance sideways and saw a man from my church a few rows down. I beat a hasty retreat out of the tent. It wasn't until years later it occurred to me that he shouldn't have been in there either.

But, that wasn't the traumatic part.

After hours of fun, corn dogs, cotton candy and all sorts of new adventures, I went to the predetermined meeting place where Daddy and Mama and the others were waiting. The folks had a real surprise for us. Daddy gave each of us another dollar and told us that we could go and buy a souvenir to take home with us. I knew immediately what I wanted to buy. I had earlier seen a place that sold helium balloons and since I'd never had one, I headed straight for that booth. They were the "balloon inside a balloon" kind. The outer one was pear shaped and the inside one was shaped like Mickey Mouse ears! I'd never seen anything so beautiful! They sold for exactly one dollar so I handed the man my bill and selected a blue one. Then I headed back to our meeting spot with a death grip on the string.

We loaded the six of us up in the old pick up and headed back to Shell Bluff. My brother Urb had bought a water gun with his dollar and couldn't wait to get back home to fill it up.

Once we got home Urb and I walked out to the edge of the field a few hundred feet from the house. We didn't have indoor plumbing so we walked out there to "take care of business" so to speak. That's when I faced a dilemma. I had to figure out a way to hold on to the string of my treasure and still maneuver my zipper.

I came up with what I thought was a brilliant idea.

I clamped the string between my teeth and got on with the task. That's when the trauma began. Somewhere during the process Urb said something to me that to this day I suspect he knew I would respond to.

"Wow! Look at that full moon!"

Well, when I opened my ten year old mouth to respond, that mystical toy escaped my grasp and began to float up into the sky. It was a very clear night and I watched as it made it's way skyward, never to be seen again. I was devastated and it didn't help that my big brother was laughing hysterically. I cried all the way back to the house and until I went to bed.

I never knew if my brother did what he did on purpose. I DO know that later, whenever he would shoot me with the water pistol that he got at the fair, he would shade his eyes and pretend to be scanning the sky looking for my balloon.

I still get a little sad when I see one of those Mickey Mouse balloons.

Among The Trees |

The Woods.

That's what we called the thousands of acres of forest that surrounded our homeplace.

There were plenty of fields of course and, over time, Daddy persuaded many hundreds of new acres of trees to become fertile planting grounds with the help of three strong sons toting, piling and burning stumps.

But there were still plenty of places to roam where the stream beds and ridges were swaddled with trees of all kinds. Oak. Pine. Maple. Cypress. God certainly exalted the Blessed South when He flung down the forested mix, along with plenty of sweetgums, hickories and hollies added for good measure.

Thus, The Woods, and all the adventures that Southern country boys could possibly dream up.

Out in the woods near where I live there was once a huge sawdust pile. One particular day the massive heap of wood chips was serving as the final citadel in our continuing make believe war against the Yankee hordes. None of us would suspend our dignity and volunteer to be northerners though, so we resorted to just throwing bark and sawdust at each other. Somebody found an old Indian grinding stone that had been dredged up during the milling. The smooth rock made a tolerable cannon ball so somebody hurled it up the side of the pile. Unfortunately, cousin Davy was directly in the line of fire and caught the missile squarely in the family jewels. He was in considerable pain, but miraculously, he went on to father several kids later in life.

Most of our woods games involved warfare of some sort, after all we are of Scottish descent, and pine thickets provided the perfect place and an abundance of weaponry. Pines cones by the thousands. Many Sunday afternoons sides were chosen, battle lines were drawn and screechy, pre-pubescent Rebel Yells emitted from a dozen boy kids and one tomboy girl. It was all great fun till somebody got hit in the eye. A scratched cornea. Cousin Davy again, poor kid. Individual family whuppings occurred with the Daddies doing the honors because, of course, we'd been told repeatedly not to throw pine cones.

Vines flourish all over the South and were utilized in our woodland escapades. We all idolized Tarzan so we'd create our own bows and spears, make up our own jungle names and spend hours swinging through the trees and over gullies on the thick natural ropes. Even back then it seemed almost surreal to watch TiLi The Jungle Boy with his flaming red hair and wearing Bermuda shorts and paisley surfer shirt riding a vine over a gorge shrieking his best ape call.

An abundance of fallen trees, not yet rotten and still sturdy, provided walls for our forts. The structures became The Alamo against Santa Anna. Fort Apache against the flaming arrows of the attacking Indians. Fort Sumter against, once again, Yankee interlopers.

Woods activities were unlimited.

We crossed snake infested swamps wearing nothing but cut off blue jeans and never gave a thought to the copperheads or cottonmouths. Until we actually saw one slither by. Then we became log walkers, timbermen of the Mighty Mississippi, until we reached dry land again.

Hide and Seek contests lasted all day long and some hiding places were never located and never revealed.

We wouldn't come home till the Mamas yelled out the back doors or the Daddies sounded the horns on the old trucks.

Later in life, in the teen years, the woods served a new purpose, though with considerably less success.

Having no clue where the local lover's lane was located, driving a few hundred feet into the darkness of the trees provided somewhere to attempt to sneak a smooch and risk a slap. Of course my nervousness during those forays, something akin to a cat after ten espressos, and the girl's inevitable, or maybe feigned, fear of the dark, rendered those fleeting moments calamitous at best.

I learned I was better at playing Davy Crockett as a ten year old in the woods than I was at playing Don Juan as a teenager.

Over the years I made sure that my own kids got to experience life in the family woods. They have built their own camps and have hiked over every acre. My son has cooked and eaten squirrels on a spit over an open fire. All three of them know the local trails as well as I do.

And at some point each of them has disappeared into the trees on the four-wheeler or on foot with a sweetheart in tow and didn't come out until I yelled out the back door or sounded the horn on my truck.

Some things never change.

In The Woods.

Billy And The Mama Pig |

Our old barn was a place of great adventure. It was huge and already ancient by the time I came along. It was made of weathered wood with a rusty tin roof.

The barn took on many incarnations.

When we were pirates on the high seas the barn was our tall ship. When refighting the Civil War it was our fort against the Yankees. Cowboys and Indians saw the barn become a mountainside with caves and canyons to hide in.

Little boys have big imaginations.

The top of the barn was the hay loft and held stacks of baled peanut straw that we fed the stock.

Before Daddy switched to strictly dirt farming we kept a few animals. Some cows. Several pigs. A yard full of chickens.

And one old goat.

His name was Billy, the same name given to every boy goat I ever knew. This particular goat I considered to be my pet. He wasn't overly friendly and was somewhat standoffish from the other creatures but I liked him anyway.

Billy spent most of his time in the barnyard. Other than the chickens who came and went whenever and wherever they pleased, Billy was the only animal that spent much time there.

On that same end of the barn was another enclosure. It was the pig pen and was separated from the barnyard by a four foot high wall with large openings into the pen.

There was once a real live hog stampede when one of us made the mistake of getting the buckets of corn to them when they were way beyond hungry.

Famished pigs can be quite aggressive.

Occasionally one of the roosters would decide it was time to act like a rooster and would chase somebody around the yard for awhile.

But for the most part, the animals appeared to live together in semi perfect harmony.

That idyllic fantasy ended for me one Spring day.

My big brother and I were in the barnyard with Billy when, for reasons known only to the goat, he decided to jump the barn wall into the pig pen. At the time, there was a large sow, a mama pig, living in the pen with a litter of newborns.

It was not a good time for Billy to get curious about what was on the other side of the wall.

I was close by and saw him crouching, getting ready to bound over the wall. I lunged toward him and grabbed him by the tail just as he went over.

That was a mistake.

Goats don't have much of a tail and what little they do have is not pleasantly located. Goats don't smell good from any angle but when you're in close proximity to that end of one, the results can be disturbing, more so when they're scared.

As soon as Billy's hooves hit the ground the sow clamped her huge jaws down on his neck, just behind his ears. Suddenly I was in a tug of war hanging over the top of the wall with most of my body in the pen! When Urb saw what was happening he grabbed the seat of my overalls and tried to pull me out, all the while yelling for me to let go of Billy's tail.

"I can't let go! She'll eat Billy!" I yelled back.

It must have been quite a spectacle, Billy being chomped on at one end by the mama pig, me holding on to the other end, and Urb hanging on to me.

About that time Daddy appeared. He picked up a stick of wood and swatted the sow on the rump.

She immediately turned loose of Billy allowing him to break my grasp. Then my brother's strength gave out, or he let me go intentionally, I never knew which, and I fell face down into the muck.

You would think that Billy would have been appreciative of my noble gesture.

Nope.

Unscathed, he stepped on the back of my neck pushing me further down into the nastiness and vaulted back out right over Urb who was by now laying on the ground, the clean, dry side, howling with laughter.

Billy was no longer my pet.

I raised up my head wondering how I could possibly regain my dignity, and looked directly into the face of the still snarling sow. My leap getting out was not as graceful as Billy's I'm certain, but leap I did.

I don't remember what became of Billy or the pig. Times were hard back then so for all I know they both ended up on the dinner table.

That was just fine with me.

GROOVIN' |

Thinking back on it, I still get a slight tremble.

I was a typical country boy. Most of the kids I'd grown up with on Rural Route 2 shared the same fear, a fear of something new and unknown. Something that we, in our wildest imaginations, could not begin to think about doing.

What made the trepidation even more intense, was knowing that, to be done correctly, "it" had to be done with the complete cooperation of a girl.

With a girl!

Growing up in the country, most of the girls we knew were kin. Sisters or cousins. There were a handful of girls at church but the very idea of participating in this particular activity with any of them was inconceivable.

How could we possibly look them in the eyes on Sunday after they had seen us that way?

Unthinkable!

No, if we were going to do the deed, it would have to be with town girls. Of course to my little gang, people who didn't live on Route 2 were town folks. We had no idea that many of our schoolmates were off the farms, just like us, just from other far reaches of the huge county.

We also knew that we couldn't avoid it forever. We lived in a new and enlightened world and certain things were just expected.

We would just have to suck it up. We would give it a go. We would learn.

To dance.

There's that shiver again from across the years.

No matter what era you learned to dance in, you probably felt the same way. Unless you were gifted with the natural ability to "trip the light fantastic" you did, at some point, feel silly or embarrassed.

Dancing was something we saw on TV, not something we'd ever done outside the confines of our homes. Oh sure, we might boogie to the old vinyl records in our living rooms when nobody else was looking. But gyrating, spinning and shaking in the presence of the fairer sex?

Meeting Lucifer face to face could not have caused as much consternation.

I managed to reach my thirteenth birthday without ever dancing outside the old farmhouse.

Mama changed all that.

She decided that I should have a big birthday party and invite my school friends. That was okay with me, as long as I didn't have to dance. She secured the old scout hut and invited forty kids from school.

I was having a great time, eating cake and ice cream, visiting with the city slickers, playing games.

And not dancing.

At some point I'm convinced that Mama conspired with a pretty girl whose daddy had taken out my tonsils a few years earlier and would later get my appendix. I say conspired because up to that point the young lady had never given me the time of day. So when she asked me to dance I nearly broke out in hives. But, ever the young Southern gentleman, I agreed.

We went to the middle of the dance floor just as somebody put on a Kingsman record.

"**Louie, Louie. Oh baby now, we gotta go...**"

I decided on the spot to just do what everybody else was doing.

Step there. Turn that way. Wiggle that body part. Move to the beat.

Oh wow! I got it! I got rhythm!

This was fun! This was great! This was rock and roll!

I danced to every song for the next hour then decided to take a break just as a slow song began.

" Lonely, I'm Mister Lonely..."

I felt a tap on my shoulder. My knees turned to jelly. It was Joanne, a girl a year younger than me who I liked. She wanted to slow dance with me. I suddenly hoped that I hadn't forgotten to use the Ban roll on. I still wasn't a great dancer but I could sweat like a July fugitive.

Somehow I got through the dance without soaking her and it turned out to be the best three minutes of my young life up to then. Before the music ended I'd developed a crush on her that lasted for...well...till now, though I haven't laid eyes on her for decades.

I learned on that long ago milestone birthday that dancing was invented for two reasons.

First, so that boys, or men, can fall unabashedly in love with girls.

Secondly, to assure the male species that we, as human beings free on the Earth, have a God given, absolute, inalienable right to make total and complete fools of ourselves while taking that glorious tumble.

I've done both a thousand times between Joanne and whoever's next.

May the dance, sweat and all, never end.

The Unexpected Prey |

Coon hunts with Daddy and Mister Chester were some of the highlights of my young life.

I got to stay up late. I got to tag along with the men and the older boys, my big brother and Mr. Chester's two sons. I got to romp around in the woods, my favorite place to this day.

I was never happier than when I was with that group tramping through the swamps and sloughs listening to the dogs trail.

Mister Chester had two dogs that he seemed especially fond of, Sarge and Toby. Seems Toby was named after Mister Chester's brother.

Or maybe it was the other way around.

Anyway, my job, as the youngest of the group, was to run under the tree after the coon was shot and fight the dogs off the kill. Armed only with a weak flashlight, I took the task very seriously.

One night, when I was around eight, we were hunting at a place called Sweetwater. Toby and Sarge treed at the edge of a field near the river. We all ran to the spot and shined our lights into the thick foliage until we spotted eyes staring back at us.

Somebody fired. Our prey fell.

I rushed in.

My light was getting dimmer but I spotted a tail sticking out of the bushes.

Being under the assumption that my hunting party would only be shooting at raccoons, I naturally believed that the tail I located was attached to just that, a raccoon.

That was an unfortunate miscalculation.

With one mighty yank I dislodged from the undergrowth one full grown mephitis mephitis.

That's the biological name for a furry little animal otherwise known as a pole cat.

A skunk.

It has several other names but at that particular moment names didn't matter. Because when I held it up the offending anatomy of the perpetrator was aimed directly at my face.

Time stood still for a few seconds as I realized exactly what was about to happen.

"This ain't no coon", I intelligently and correctly deduced to myself.

Then, with his last defiant effort the skunk did what skunks do.

I caught the full blast.

As the rancid cloud engulfed me I did the only thing that I knew to do. I dropped the reeking mess and lit out across the field like a bat out of Hades as though I could outrun the vapors.

No such luck.

Daddy and Mister Chester still didn't know what had happened. They told me later that they thought I'd been bitten by a rabid coon. When I took off they started chasing me across the peanut patch. Normally, either of them could have caught me easily but panic gave me wings and I was flying. Finally Daddy got close enough to grab my collar.

He immediately regretted that he had.

When he inhaled he fully grasped the situation and, being the compassionate father, let go of me, backed off about twenty yards and ordered me to stay where I was.

I was wailing but Daddy assured me that nobody had ever died from stinking to High Heaven.

The situation seemed dire to me but everybody else was howling.

From a distance.

Once they stopped laughing they decided on a course of action. Everybody started toward the truck with me tagging along a goodly piece behind them.

Downwind of course.

Back at the truck Daddy had me strip down to my drawers and built a little campfire with my clothes. He found an old burlap seed sack in the bed of the truck. He split the sack open and wrapped it around me, then put me in the back of the truck where I rode home.

Fifteen miles of mostly rutted dirt roads in the bed of an old pickup on a cold night swaddled in nothing but baggy boxers and a scratchy croker sack.

It wasn't very comfortable.

When we got home Mama scrubbed me with Lava soap under a hose pipe in the back yard.

I wasn't allowed inside till I smelled better.

The dogs wouldn't play with me for days.

My siblings were suddenly armed with plenty of ammunition for my humiliation.

I can laugh about it now of course.

Looking back on the incident over the years it's still hard to comprehend that such a cute little fuzz ball with such a tiny little posterior could produce such putridity.

But even at the risk of another spraying, I'd give anything for one more chance to be in those woods with Daddy and Mister Chester hearing the hounds bay.

Just with a little more wisdom and a better functioning flashlight.

BEING COOL |

Growing up in the South, in the sixties, there was one thing that was of utmost importance to me and to most kids my age.

The quest to be cool.

Cool is one of the few slang words that has retained its meaning over the years.

"She's a cool gal", or "Those are really cool shoes", meant pretty much the same thing back then as they do now.

Everybody wanted to be cool. Some of us struggled with the journey more than others.

Somewhere along the way I grew some great sideburns, thick and bright red. They looked cool but then everybody grew sideburns and the luster wore off.

I played football and was pretty good at it, so, for three months in the Fall, I was one of the cool guys. I won a letter jacket. It looked cool but could only be worn a few months each year.

But to me, the epitome of coolness was having a great car.

I knew that I would get a car when I turned sixteen because Daddy bought us cars at that age as payment for working on the farm, so I fantasized for years about my first car.

I had dreams of something sleek, shiny and fast. Something cool.

That dream died the day Daddy drove up in a pea green

Rambler Hornet, got out, and handed me the keys. It was about as uncool a vehicle as America has ever produced. Three speed, column shift. No radio. No air conditioning. No fancy wheels.

And NO chance of ever picking up girls.

But, it was transportation and I decided immediately to make the most of it. I knew that I would never be able to drag race on Quaker road, but I thought, if it can't be cool, I'd at least make it sound cool.

I'd heard of something called glass pack mufflers. To this day I don't know exactly what glass pack means, but I knew it made cars sound cool. So I saved my money and bought one.

Being a poor mechanic and not being particularly fond of laying on my back under a car, it took me several hours to get the new muffler installed, but I finally completed the task. I climbed into the car and cranked the engine.

The deep rumbling was totally cool!

I cleaned up and got ready to go to town. I drove straight to Danny's Dairy Bar where all of the cool kids, well, actually where ALL the kids hung out. I made a couple of circles around the place and some of my friends actually took notice of the new sound and came over to congratulate me. I had managed to turn the Hornet into an at least acceptable sounding machine. Still not pretty, but acceptable. That was an accomplishment.

My friend Mike left his car and got into mine. We cruised the length of town to the lake then headed back to the Dairy Bar.

Back then, if you didn't have a car with enough power to spin the tires and burn rubber, the alternative was the "back it down" maneuver. You put the car in reverse, backed up as fast as you could, then jerked the car into first gear. When the tires reversed you would get a fairly decent screech.

I knew that the Hornet was capable of the move because I'd practiced it on the dirt roads out in the country.

Unfortunately, I hadn't tried it since I installed the glass pack.

When we drove back into the Dairy Bar Mike dared me to "back it down" right there in the parking lot.

I threw the car into reverse, sped backward, then slammed it into first gear. The car lurched forward with the tires spinning, actually burning rubber.

I was in coolness heaven!

Until the new muffler fell off.

Suddenly my cool sounding Hornet roared like a pulp wood truck.

This was definitely not cool and that fact was reinforced by the sounds of howling laughter from nearby teens and from Mike who quickly abandoned me since my car was no longer cool either.

I decided to retreat. I jumped out, opened the truck and grabbed the cursed muffler. That was a mistake. Who knew mufflers got hot? It wasn't hot when I put it on.

My sizzling hands only increased the laughter and I was losing coolness by the second.

I grabbed a rag, got the muffler into the trunk and headed back to Shell Bluff. Glancing at the blisters starting to form on my fingers I had only one thought.

" I wonder if Mama will let me skip school until football season?"

Life's Little Replays |

Recently while going through some boxes that I had neglected since my last move, I came across my framed college degree that I had earned all those years ago, something that I have never displayed but of which I am very proud.

Seeing it brought to mind a long ago conversation with my high school guidance counselor. When I told her that I wanted to go to college she pointedly replied that I was not college material, that I would never make it through college and that I should go to trade school. Over the years I have wished that I could go back and tell her what I really thought about that.

Then I began thinking about some other things and events that I would like to revisit during that same era of my life. Nothing earth shattering or history changing, just a few minor "do overs".

I remember sitting in an algebra class taught by a woman who we affectionately referred to as The Duck. All math was agony for me but this was the worst.

We were given a problem that went something like this:

" If an eastbound train leaves Chicago for New York City at 7:10 PM and travels 55 miles per hour for 13 hours, and if Johnny spends three dollars and forty-seven cents at the store and pays with a ten dollar bill, what is the square root of Einstein's theory of irregularity?"

That might be a little bit off, but that's how I remember it.

Given another shot, here's how I would answer.

"I don't give a monkey's fanny, and, given an extra lifetime I still wouldn't be able to get it right. Furthermore, I've been to the future and I can report that never in human history has anybody actually needed to know!"

That's what I'd tell The Duck. Then I'd apologize for me and all the other kids who quacked every time she turned her back.

Then I'd go back to the week when an inept football coach had actually done some scouting and knew that our next opponent would be running a short screen pass play to my side. He drilled it into me for days, "Go out and bat it down. Bat it down! Do not try to catch it!"

Game day. Sure enough, they ran the play. I floated out. The ball came right to me. I reached up and batted it down. Easy play. I looked back. The receiver had slipped down ten yards away. The goal line was fifteen yards in the other direction.

Even a big, slow lineman like me could have scored easily. My only chance to do something other than block and tackle.

"*Do NOT try to catch it!*"

My do over? Intercept. Score. Go to the sideline and hand the ball to the beloved coach along with a suggestion as to where he could stick it.

Next, I might ask that dark haired beauty two years older than me to go to a dance. Of course this is the do over version of me. The sixteen year old me could only sweat and hyperventilate around her. Now I know humiliation only lasts a few days. What did I have to lose?

In my replay world I would resist the temptation to smoke that first Marlboro, a habit I didn't kick for several years.

I would thank Mrs. Tinley for encouraging me to write and for showing me how much fun it can be. Sadly, I can't tell her now.

I might even try to warn Juddy and Beep and Sharon and a few others about certain people and places and times to avoid. They might have gotten to be with us longer.

I would certainly NOT attempt the back down maneuver at the Dairy Bar with a loose muffler.

Nothing that I would do would change much about worldly events. Just a tweak here and there.

And that high school guidance counselor? Here's what I'd say to her knowing what I know now.

I would say, "You were right. I wasn't college material. I loved going to college, hated going to class. If it rained I skipped because it was raining. If it was sunny I skipped so I could go to the lake. I'm still not sure where the library is at the university. But, I did graduate, fair and square. I packed my four year degree into five and a half years and went out to take on the world. So, thank you for your trade school advice but, I had a lot more fun doing it my way".

That's what I'd tell her.

Some things don't need to be changed.

Mud Farming |

I'm not a farmer.

Farm boy yes. Farmer no.

I grew up on a farm. Worked on a farm. Probably even looked like a farmer. But even when I lived on the farm I was mostly a weed puller and stump toter.

Not a farmer.

I really do love being out in the fields. I like the smell of newly turned soil and the feel of the soft dirt underfoot. I enjoy watching crops grow and mature.

But I had to admit to myself long ago that trying to rip a living out of the sandy earth on our place was not how I wanted to amass my fortune.

Nope. Definitely not a farmer.

If Daddy were alive he would vouch for that fact and would point to any number of examples as proof.

Like the time I lost control of the tractor I was driving and tore down thirty feet of fence. I was only eight, but still.

Or the times when I committed farming felonies known as " eight row lightning strikes". Those happen when you're plowing a field with an eight row cultivator and, for reasons known only to God, the tractor eases a bit off the row and the plows cut the roots of the plants under the soil killing the crops for a few yards until you get the iron beast back in line. The murder of the plants is not immediately evident but after a few days perfect patterns of brown, dead crops, exactly eight rows wide appear among the greenery. Whenever that happened Daddy would have to determine which one of his fine sons was the last to plow.

More often than not it was me.

One thing that I didn't mind doing on the farm was harrowing. It was relatively easy compared to plowing, where you couldn't for one nanosecond allow the tractor to waver. Or to running a cotton picker or peanut thrasher where there were all kinds of misadventures that could befall an agriculturally challenged kid like me.

Harrowing was not precise.

All you had to do was let the disks down on one end of a field, drive to the other end while the harrow did its thing, raise the implement up, turn the tractor around and repeat the process.

It was simple. Not much could go wrong.

Right.

One day Daddy sent me off quite a distance from the home place to harrow up a field to get it ready for Spring planting. He warned me about a mud hole on one end of the field. He told me exactly where it was and to avoid it. When I got to the field I scouted out the spot so that I'd know in plenty of time when I was getting close to the wet area. By no means did I want to bog down.

Harrowing is also comparatively mindless work allowing a young boy too much time to daydream. Which is exactly what I was doing when, after a couple of hours of disking, I drove straight into that mud hole and sunk the huge right tire up to the axle.

" This is not good", I thought to myself.

I tried really hard to get the tractor unstuck. Not a chance. I just made it worse.

I walked about a mile to the closest house and called home hoping Mama would answer. Daddy never answered the phone. Until that day. He hollered up a blue storm but he came to the field and after much digging, sweating and cussing we got the tractor out.

Daddy headed home. I saw him driving out of the field onto the road just as I wheeled the tractor around.

Too close. I dropped the same tire into the same mud hole, just pointed a different direction.

Suddenly I faced a very difficult decision.

Should I walk off into the woods and hide there the rest of my life? I was a boy scout for a while, I could eat animals and berries. Or do I call Daddy again?

I actually headed toward the river and started trying to recall how to construct rabbit snares before I changed my mind.

I called Daddy. He came back. He didn't yell or cuss. He just kept shaking his head and mumbling, no doubt lamenting whatever cruel trick of fate made me his progeny.

He eventually forgave me and when I told him that I didn't want to farm but wanted to go to college he was mightily relieved. He ardently encouraged me to seek another vocation.

My farming career ended before the advent of the sixteen row cultivator.

Mercifully.

One Little Arson |

It was just a little yard fire.

Of course "little" is in the eye of the beholder.

I did everything right.

I waited until the woods were wet from the recent rains.

I waited till there was no wind.

I got a burn permit.

Number 4038.

I followed all the rules.

So I was a little surprised when two fire pumpers rumbled up in the yard accompanied by a fire captain in an SUV.

Okay, so the fire could be seen from over a mile away. It was totally contained.

My young buddy Joshua stopped by too. He spotted the fire and, like a good neighbor, came to check on me.

He thought the homeplace was burning.

I was appreciative. Good neighbors are like gold.

But there was really no need.

You see, I am an experienced firestarter.

And safely beyond the statute of limitations.

I passed a polygraph exam for police academy when the question was posed:

"Have you, in the past ten years, been charged with or

convicted of any crime?"

"No", I replied.

Only yes or no answers are allowed so I didn't have to expound on the fact that I HAD perpetrated one questionable act slightly outside of the designated decade.

I once worked for a demolition company tearing down an old rail station where a civic center now resides.

The lot was several city blocks long and just as wide. Out in the middle was a site where an old building had been razed. All that was left was the concrete basement. The cavity had been filled with broken boards and timbers from the old depot.

The pile was bigger than a two story house.

It would have taken weeks to haul the wood away.

One Friday afternoon the foreman, Paul, said, to no one in particular, " If somebody would set that big pile of wood on fire over the weekend, that somebody might find an extra twenty dollars in his pay envelope next week".

I took the bait.

I wanted the extra cash but I also had an ulterior motive.

Saturday night I talked my cousin EJ into going with me. I dressed in all black clothes. Even a black skull cap.

EJ dropped me off on one side of the huge lot, then drove to the predetermined pick up site.

I ran to the pile, which was over a quarter mile from any house or building, lit a railroad flare, jammed it deep into the splintered wood, then went to the other side and did the same thing.

I sprinted for the car thinking it would never work.

No way was it going to catch and burn.

But, just in case, we hightailed it. We went to a bar across the river where I committed my second crime of the night since I was under twenty-one.

Just a bit of youthful imprudence.

Later I picked up my brand new girlfriend. A city girl with a country mile wide smile. Eyes so blue that I could never describe them until years later when I swam in the warm waters of the South Pacific the first time.

I'd met her on a teen trip to Colorado.

I was smitten.

I wanted to show her my handiwork. I still wasn't certain that the massive pile had ignited but I was hoping my feat might impress her.

As we rounded the corner near the lot, suddenly the whole sky was ablaze. Flames towered a hundred feet. A half dozen firetrucks were futilely pumping water onto the pile which was nothing more than a fat lighter inferno.

It was impressive but we didn't hang around long for obvious reasons.

First thing Monday morning a suspicious fire chief paid us a visit.

If the chief had glanced at me my petrified look would have betrayed me as the arsonist and I'd have gone straight to the bighouse.

"I'm guessing lightning struck it," drawled Paul, even though it hadn't stormed for weeks.

He instantly became my very favorite human being.

Nobody got hurt. All that burned was a useless pile of wood.

And I made an extra twenty bucks for my exploits.

I never found out whether my girlfriend was dazzled by my daring or stunned by my stupidity. She never actually said one way or the other. But I noticed later that she had married another guy, presumably not a pyromaniac, to whom she is still happily wed.

Perhaps girls are unimpressed by felonious behavior.

Even so, her smile made it worth a go.

In retrospect, it was not a brilliant thing to do and I would never encourage such behavior.

Never.

Unless you're eighteen and the ulterior motive has ocean blue eyes.

APPARITION |

It was a dark and stormy night.

Yes, I know that line has been used a billion times since it was first penned by a Victorian novelist.

But the night in question truly was a dark and stormy Southern night.

Halloween fell on Saturday the year my friends and I were high school seniors. That night I was hanging around the Dairy Bar with R.J. and Mike. We had won our football game the night before and were celebrating with chili dogs and milk shakes. Wheatie drifted in later and we started talking about some of the scary legends that caused us to keep flashlights in our cars. Nobody would have admitted to being afraid of the dark but being armed with illumination was just common sense.

We'd all grown up hearing about Bloody Bones, a skeletal phantom who would sneak up on unsuspecting kids, coincidentally, usually when spooky stories were being told, and scare the bejeebers out of them. Old Bloody made most of his appearances around Halloween.

We had also seen the monster movies at the old Grand Theater. Dracula. Frankenstein. The Werewolf.

Locally, we had our own murderous fiends allegedly lurking the backroads of the county, waiting for the right moment to strike.

There was the Gill Man who could suddenly arise from pretty much any body of water.

Bear Gator, a mutant cross between a black bear and an alligator.

And in our neck of the woods we had Jacob, a man at least 150 years old who we sometimes caught glimpses of in the edge of the woods, still carrying the ax with which he murdered his family in the 1800's.

None of those ever scared me.

I didn't believe in such silliness.

At least not until that long ago Halloween night when my friends and I saw something that none of us will ever forget.

The Rock Creek Fire Lady.

We sat under the overhang at the Dairy Bar trying to stay dry and look cool at the same time. The conversation had turned to the legend of the flaming lady. About then some of the girls showed up so, naturally, we dared them to go with us to Rock Creek to confront the ghost.

The four of us, along with Martha Mary, Patty and Patsi crammed into my Rambler and headed out.

The rain stopped just as we parked in the graveyard but a thick fog had rolled in. The quarter moon was trying to peek through the clouds but wasn't making any progress. An owl hooted off in the distance as if to warn us to stay out of the trees.

We made our way down the bank to the edge of the creek. Strangely, all three flashlights began to go dim as soon as we were under the canopy of the forest. We stumbled our way along the edge of the creek bumping into the cypress knees sticking out of the mud. We got tangled up in hanging vines. We splashed in the dank water of the mudflats. We raised such a racket that I was sure no respectable ghost would waste time on us.

I was wrong.

I actually felt the arrival before I saw it.

Suddenly the fog was parted by a blast of heat coming from the top of the steep bank on the opposite side of the creek. We all looked up at the same time and there it was.

The Rock Creek Fire Lady, bursting aflame against the dark sky.

Somebody screamed, one of the girls I think.

Or maybe it was me.

Anyway, for several seconds I stared at the fiery figure, paralyzed by the sight yet fascinated that it made absolutely no sound.

No sound at all.

When I snapped to and looked around I realized that I'd been abandoned and decided on the spot that being alone with that thing was not a recommended course of action.

I lit out for the car. I think the ghost chased me for a ways but I outran her.

I also passed R.J., the fastest boy on our team, like he was crawling. I conferred with him as to what had become of the rest of our party and we made another spot decision that they were on their own.

Not to worry. All of them beat us back to the Hornet.

We piled in and freighted fannies back to town.

You can believe this tale if you want. That's up to you. But if you go looking for the Rock Creek Fire Lady, I recommend you take reliable flashlights, good running shoes and a few good friends.

And a healthy imagination.

Making The Grade |

I never claimed to be a good student.

During my college years I crammed my four year degree into five and a half years, but, I still managed to graduate from the world's finest institution of higher learning, The University of Georgia.

I got the diploma but it didn't come easy.

Daydreaming nearly full time and studying almost never does not sum up to a sterling grade point average.

If I could have majored in daydreaming I'd almost certainly hold at least one doctorate.

Doctor of Inattentiveness?

My sister SherryLou came to see me recently and brought me something she'd found that documented my checkered academic history.

My ninth grade report card.

It was faded and wrinkled but one glance took me back decades to a time when the scholarly standard that I set for myself was to make good enough grades to remain eligible to play football and to stay in Mama's good graces, in that order.

Lofty goals indeed.

To say that I hated schoolwork would be a vast understatement.

Math and science classes made me dizzy. Geography bored me to numbness. English seemed like such an obvious waste of time since I already spoke my own version of the language.

But there was one oasis of learning in the desert wasteland that I had to endure every school day. A place where my young brain was never stretched beyond it's self imposed limits.

Shop.

I loved shop class, at least most of it.

Shortly before Sis brought me the old report card I came across the bookcase that I built as my shop project so long ago. It had lived in a closet at Mama's house for years.

The reappearance of the bookcase and the old report card made me quite sentimental.

The bookcase was made of white pine, one by twelve lumber, stained dark cherry and triple varnished. I built it, got a decent grade, then brought it home and presented it to my folks. Daddy took one look and stifled a horselaugh but Mama made a nice, obligatory fuss over it.

Finding my wooden creation made me nostalgic.

Coach Buck's shop class was a respite from the daily grind of a curriculum that made me almost prefer pulling weeds or toting stumps on the farm to sitting in those torturous old desks that were designed for humans half my size.

Coach Buck let us build things and repair other things and generally tinker around with tools I'd personally never laid eyes on before. He was a good teacher but he wouldn't tolerate the misuse or abuse of shop equipment.

One day, for reasons lost to history, I allowed myself to give in to a dare that I could drill a hole through a two by four using a countersink bit, a serious deviation from it's intended purpose. I was working away with the hand held brace and bit, surrounded by my darers, when I sensed an extra pair of eyes watching me.

Coach Buck's eyes.

That was a time before parents who were so protective of their little darlings made school paddlings a criminal act. And Coach Buck was not at all discriminatory. All the co-conspirators to my maltreatment of his tools joined me in receiving an epic butt whuppin'.

His paddle could lift you off the floor and it didn't matter how much Blue Horse notebook paper you stuffed in your back pockets, it stung.

That part wasn't fun, but, except for those rare but well earned sessions of corporal punishment, I looked forward to the sounds of the power tools, the smell of the woodworking and the feel of sawdust underfoot.

I truly loved shop class.

The only problem, I was, at best, a fair to middling craftsmen.

The proof was there in all it's splendor for me to see.

My bookcase was pitiful.

Especially when I compared it to one, more prominently displayed at Mama's house, that Willie made under the supervision of Coach Buck a few years later. His has shelves and doors and ornamental hinges.

The side by side contrast made me considerably less sentimental about my work of artlessness.

So, when I moved, I tossed it into the fire with all the other junk I had no further use for. I didn't want any of my kids to have to endure having it in their home, telling their friends that I made it and pretending to cherish it.

With the evidence gone up in smoke, through the years, I can describe my work anyway I want to.

Some things are better left to the wistful imagination.

I did keep the old report card though.

For the record, Coach Buck gave me almost a B in shop.

But the memories are grade A.

II
THE FAMILY

None but a mule denies his family.

~Arabian Proverb ~

CERTIFIABLE |

Late one evening, around midnight, I was standing in a clearing in the woods howling at the sky.

Oh, don't even act like you've never done the same thing yourself!

Some might consider such actions to border on insanity but I had a perfectly legitimate reason.

It was a full moon.

I come from a long line of crazy folks.

Not all insane people in the Blessed South are kin to me, but all my kinfolk are insane.

Every last one of them. Even the in-laws.

It's not a new condition, bred into my clan through intermarrying with the other longstanding loony families around these parts, though undoubtedly certain unions added to the madness.

And it can't be totally blamed on the pressures and burdens of modern life since there are documented incidents from many years ago that prove my hypothesis.

I suspect genetics.

You want proof? I've got plenty.

I have a long dead distant cousin who was a master carpenter. During his colorful and storied lifetime, he was purported to be as mean as a snake and just as unpredictable.

He once beat the mailbox into oblivion when the postman delivered a bill he wasn't happy to see.

According to one legend, this cousin was on the roof of a house that he was building when a storm blew in. Even with thunder booming and lightening slashing all around he refused to leave the roof. Soaking wet, he stood up, held his hammer straight toward the sky in one hand while shaking his other fist at the thunderheads, shouting into the gales, daring the lightening to strike him down.

If that ain't crazy grits ain't groceries.

Another relative, a great aunt many years gone now, was often referred to as eccentric.

Early in the last century she gave birth to a baby girl. Nearly two years later she and her little family welcomed a new baby boy. Then, for reasons known only to God and forever unexplained, she decided that the two year old girl and the newborn boy were, in fact, twin girls. She began dressing them alike and introducing them as twins, though it was never clear how she accounted for the obvious size difference.

Even the written genealogical records of the family state that her only children were twins.

I'd say that falls a nut or two beyond eccentric.

Incidentally, in spite of that early forced cross dressing, or perhaps because of it, that male cousin turned out to be very manly and not the least bit effeminate, later becoming a record setting athlete who fought in World War Two.

A cousin, who is the best mechanic in Dixie, once put a powerful V8 engine into a Volkswagen bug. He'd tear down the side streets in town, rubber burning and loud mufflers roaring with the express purpose of alerting the local police. By the time they arrived looking for the offender, he would have parked the unassuming looking little car and would be sitting behind the wheel looking as innocent as a schoolboy, drinking a Coke.

He fooled them for years and never got caught, at least not for that particular stunt.

Another relative allegedly gardens in the nude though I have no proof of that fact and pray I never see any. The mental image alone is enough to bring on night tremors. He does assure me that he is particularly careful when using the rototiller.

One of my brothers thought it was hilarious to load up his raggedy Blazer with half of our family's male lineage, find an old trail that went straight and steep down to the river, go flying downhill then slam on the questionably reliable brakes at the last second. Have you ever heard eight grown men scream like eight little girls? It's not a pretty sound. On more than one occasion, a few more inches would have meant that you wouldn't be reading this and at least a dozen children, mine included, would have never been born cause all their crazy future daddies drowned in the Savannah.

The only thing crazier than the near death experience itself was all eight kinsmen yelling " Let's do it again!" as soon as we caught our collective breaths.

Every last one. Crazy.

So the next time it's a full moon and you're standing in your own clearing contemplating a loud, wolfish chat with the moon, don't give a second thought to whether somebody might hear you and think you're nuts.

Cause you are. Just accept it like we do in my family.

Happy howling.

Uncle Cuz |

He is the consummate Southern Gentleman.

Anyone who knows him well would agree.

He's been married to his Southern Belle for close to six decades and still treats her with respect and kindness. He teamed up with her to raise four rowdy boys and two girlie girls and has watched all of them evolve into hardworking, patriotic Southern citizens.

Six ornery, opinionated chips off the old block.

Said with sincere affection.

Actually, those traits afflicted ninety-nine percent of the females and one hundred percent of the males in our family.

But that's another story.

This man, one of my all time favorite relatives, was also a successful businessman, is an adored granddaddy to several grandkids and is a friend to literally thousands of people from all over.

He's also an ex-Marine, though he'll remind you right quick, once a Marine always a Marine.

He would say that the most important aspect of his life has been his walk with the Lord. He has been a pillar of his church forever and has devoted his life to that journey. You won't have a five minute conversation with him without getting a mini Bible lesson, sometimes serious scriptural exegesis, sometimes a little milk and honey.

I feel certain that he would pshaw the above described praise saying that the roles he has filled are nothing more than a man doing what a man is supposed to do.

He won't like reading about himself here.

But nobody I've ever known is more deserving of admiration. Uncle Julian.

I rarely mention real names, in order to protect the guilty, but exceptions can be made for exceptional folk.

He's really not my uncle. He's my first cousin but is considerably older than me. I call him Uncle out of pure, unadulterated respect.

I'd take a whipping before I'd call him by his first name and, in my growing up years, Daddy would have provided one if he'd heard me do it.

Southerners respect our elders and my Uncle serves us as an elder in the true sense of the word.

You know the kind of person I'm referring to if you are from a large Southern family. You have cousins, or uncles and aunts, or even some relatives of uncertain but unquestionably accepted kinship, who you hold in nearly revered positions.

It's a Southern thang yall.

My family often gathers at The Pond. There's a swimming hole that's the center of that little universe.

This Uncle is not a big man. All of his sons, with one bowlegged exception, are taller than him.

In the pond he was as strong as a Jersey bull.

Many Sunday afternoons several cousins my age would gang up and try to duck him under the water. He, having not that long hence returned from the Marine Corps, would deftly fight us all off and, when he'd had enough, would hold a couple of his assailants under the water until the fight left us.

I remember on more than one occasion thinking, as I struggled to break free, lungs about to bust, that I had taken my last breath and would soon meet Jesus. Just as I began to hear angels singing he'd snatch me to the surface, toss me aside, then take on his next victim.

Years later he started a new 4th of July tradition. We would hear a loud whoop that only he could muster. He'd come rumbling down the red clay hill from the pavilion hollering all the way how hot and humid it was. Then he'd dive into The Pond fully dressed. Sometimes he'd pause to kick off his shoes. Most often not.

It was quite entertaining.

He's the one always selected to pump us up with a red, white and blue stemwinder reminding us why he is so grateful and blessed to be an American and why we all doggone well ought to be thankful too.

One year Mama had surgery and we were all in the waiting area of the hospital. I thought to myself that we should be circled up praying. My younger brother later told me that he was thinking the same thing, but neither of us suggested it.

In walked Uncle Cuz.

"Gather around yall, and let's pray," he said.

No hesitation or timidity on his part.

That's the man he is.

He's lived a life of unparalleled dignity.

I hope that I've learned something from him.

Thank you, sir, for the life lessons.

Thank you for your service to the church, the country and our family.

And thank you for not drowning me.

Semper Fi Uncle Cuz.

Author's note:

My Uncle Cuz went on to be with his Lord shortly after this article was published.

We were only able to bury the parts of him that died, the earthly remains. The man he was will never die.

Never.

Semper Fi indeed.

Mama And The Rat |

If you grew up on a farm in the South like I did, you understand why some of the ladies are as tough as the men.

It was, and still is a hard life, despite the advances in agricultural science and technology. Back when most farms were still family ventures, the wives were as important to the operation as were the men, just as they are in today's more advanced farming businesses.

For the farm kids it was also a hard life but one that most of us would not trade for any other.

My brothers and my sister and I worked harder than many kids our age but part of the reward was having thousands of acres of farm and woodlands as our playgrounds when we weren't working.

We played in the woods, in the barn and in the swamps. The tool sheds and chicken coops made wonderful forts and sailing ships for little farm boys with big dreams and bigger imaginations.

Sometimes we would also play under the house. Back then old farm houses were built up off of the ground allowing plenty of room under them to explore and to occasionally hide from Mama if it became necessary.

I'm sure that Mama spent whatever time that she wasn't doing farm work or housework either watching us, looking for us, or wondering where we were. And, even when we did try to hide, she was always able to locate us without much trouble.

I think she had kid radar.

There were times when I was sure she worked as hard as Daddy did but still had time to look after us.

I've seen her driving tractors, picking and hoeing cotton and wrestling those beat up old peanut and cotton trucks to the gin houses in town. Yet she somehow still had the time to cook three full meals a day, every day.

One day she showed us that she possessed another skill that we had never witnessed before.

She could shoot like Annie Oakley.

Daddy taught all of his kids to shoot the rifle at an early age and I guess he taught her too.

One day while we were playing in one of the side yards near a pig pen, suddenly a huge rat appeared near the fence. It was the biggest one I had ever seen before or have since.

It was as ugly as a mud fence and as big as a beagle.

That rat just stood there by that fence eating something, probably a pilfered egg from the hen house.

We all ran to the house and told Mama to come see the huge varmint. She took one look at it and went to get the .22 rifle off of the shelf where Daddy kept it.

The pig pen was probably a good 30 yards from the back porch and when Mama came out of the house with the gun that nasty thing just kept munching and paid us no attention whatsoever.

Mama stood on the back porch, took careful aim and with one shot to the head, sent that rat to his reward.

We were all so excited we ran out there and grabbed it up by the tail to bring it and show it to Mama.

When we got back to the porch Mama was standing there with tears in her eyes, crying over killing the rat.

It may have been the first time that I was ever aware of the combination of toughness and tenderness that is so vital, and is an absolute requirement in a successful Southern farm wife and mother.

Mama had it. The toughness that it took to kill an egg hunting rat and the tenderness to mourn it's passing.

Mama had both.

That's what made her Mama.

Just Sittin' Around |

A Southern front porch is the window to the world if the one sitting on it has the proper wit and imagination, and we all know that most Southerners are abundantly equipped with both those characteristics.

Folks around these parts don't lack for the conversational skills and debative temperament necessary for the preservation of the history and customs of our homeland.

In other words, put a bunch of us on a front porch with a pitcher of lemonade and there's no issue that won't be thoroughly discoursed.

There's just one small problem.

A shortage of front porches.

Sadly, most houses built in the past few decades don't have them.

Instead, there are gazebos and decks and covered patios, all nice places to gather, but very few front porches.

After all, dogs can't snooze and kids can't play under gazebos.

Decks are usually sunny, and therefore, hot.

And covered patios are normally away from the house so you have to keep going back and forth to fill up the tea glasses or check on supper.

The front porch is right there, just outside the front door.

Shady and inviting. Maybe partly screened in to keep the skeeters and gnats out but always airy and cooler than inside.

Grandma Julia had a great front porch. Her house sat on a hill overlooking the highway with a pasture in between. The porch was furnished with an assortment of unmatched rocking chairs and wingbacks and, of course, a porch swing. The front steps were huge, or at least it seemed so to me as a child.

The family spent many evenings gathered at Grandma's with the kids, dozens of cousins, sitting on the porch steps telling spooky stories or playing far flung games of hide and seek or tag. The porch was always "base" where you couldn't be tagged by whoever was "it".

Daddy and several of his brothers and brothers-in-law sat on the porch talking about farming, hunting or politics. Mostly politics. Occasionally a few of them would walk out to somebody's pick up truck where they would reach under the front seat and then stand around for a few minutes. Back then I had no idea what they went to the truck for.

Now I do.

Every now and then one of the men would call out to one of us.

"Don't eat to many of those green apples. They'll give you a bellyache," or " You tear a hole in them britches and your Mama's gonna whup your butt."

Mama and the aunts, and Grandma, were usually somewhere in the house talking about whatever women talk about, most likely the bunch of heathens sitting on the front porch. Every now and then one of them would stick their head out the screen door.

"What are yall doing out here?"

"Just sittin' around." Always the same answer.

Satisfied, the designated lady would return to the inner sanctum.

That's just the way it worked.

At some point, when the ladies decided that it was getting time to go home, they would all gradually ease on out to the front porch themselves. But instead of leaving, they'd find a chair, join in the conversation and another hour or two would pass.

I suspect that Grandma's front porch was a comfortable respite from their day to day lives. There were times when it seemed to be the center of our family's universe.

There's no telling how many engagements and wedding dates and baby announcements and all other imaginable family news flashes were announced on that porch.

The kin were always reluctant to leave at the end of the night but when the time finally did arrive, after the men had re-fought The War and solved most of the world's political difficulties, each mother would gather her brood and herd them to the car. Often, I'd have a new, previously predicted hole in the knee or seat of my jeans but Mama wouldn't whup me cause she felt sorry for me since I'd been throwing up from eating too many green apples.

Back at home, she and Daddy would put us to bed, then slip out to our own front porch with it's own porch swing to enjoy a few quiet moments alone.

To this day I can remember hearing the swings rusty chains squeak and their quiet voices as I dropped off to sleep.

You can't put a price on recollections like those but I'd spend my last dollar to hear them again.

So, when I built my house on our homeplace I included porches, two of them, long and spacious.

Plenty of room for rocking chairs and a swing.

And memory making gatherings.

Come on by and sit awhile.

A Worthy Woman |

The article was short.

Not an article at all really, more like blurb in a local information column.

"Miss Katie Bateman is visiting Miss Annie Hatcher."

It could have been written about either of my daughters and the hundreds of times they had overnight guests in our home. Little girls love "spend the night" parties.

Always have, always will.

The little lady in question, Annie, was ten years old at the time of the writing.

A later item, when Annie was twelve years old, read as follows:

"Miss Annie Hatcher returned home this week, after a two weeks visit to friends in Augusta."

Yet another gossip tidbit about the little social butterfly:

"Miss Fannie Reese, of Shell Bluff, is spending the week with Miss Annie Hatcher."

By that point Annie was thirteen years old but still a little girl, apparently with a wide circle of friends.

Move forward five years.

"Miss Annie Hatcher was married to Wm. B. Mobley at Curtis Baptist Church Wednesday evening. They will make Augusta their home."

None of the above described events shook the Earth. Little

girls are born. Little girls make friends. Little girls grow up and marry.

But these particular occurrences, as insignificant as they might appear, are noteworthy because of who "Annie" was and because of when the words were written.

Over one hundred years ago.

She was my Aunt Annie.

If you grew up in the rural South you know who Aunt Annie was. You may not have known my aunt, but you knew someone like her, a strong, cussedly independent, Southern woman.

And to my kid eyes, she was ancient.

Aunt Annie was over seventy years old when I was born and technically she was my "great" aunt.

What deems her remarkable is that more than forty years after we buried her at the age of eighty-six years old, we often still talk about her.

Her first husband, mentioned above, contracted an illness while fighting in the Spanish-American War, several years before their marriage. He never fully recovered and died a few years after the wedding leaving Aunt Annie a young widow, but before his death he built the house that she would live in all of her days.

The house still stands less than a mile from mine.

Her second marriage lasted many years but she was again widowed in her early sixties.

She lived alone for the rest of her life.

Well into her eighties Aunt Annie ran a little store just across the road from the homeplace. Just a few shelves of canned goods, candy and gum, but she ran it efficiently.

She grew and canned a garden full of vegetables every year.

She hosted Baptist Women's Missionary meetings in her tidy home on a regular basis.

Even after she lost much of her vision she was a regular pianist at the church and never missed a worship service. She didn't really play the piano, she assaulted it. She was a tiny woman but she smacked the keys hard enough for the departed ones in the graveyard to sing along.

Perhaps a human being's true earthly merit is measured by the fact that decades after their deaths, memories of them remain an important part of the family lore.

Like hearing Aunt Annie play " Listen To The Mockingbird" as often as we'd request it.

Or seeing her at war with a huge snake with nothing but a garden hoe.

Or tasting her perfect strawberries.

But folks like her leave behind much more that memories.

They pass on a legacy.

Aunt Annie sure did.

She never had children of her own but she helped raise dozens of them, me included.

She even left us with one very memorable quote.

She was once in the home of a younger woman relative and was helping clean up after a meal. The younger lady had served biscuits and was about the throw the leftover ones to the dogs.

Aunt Annie pitched a small hissy.

" A sorry woman will throw more out the back door than a good man can bring in the front door."

Try getting away with that kind of country wisdom in the politically correct times we live in.

Whoever that "sorry" woman was has been lost to history but I'm sure Aunt Annie was not as concerned about hurting her feelings as she was about wasted food. And I'm certain that the biscuits found their way back onto the table at a future meal.

Aunt Annie.

Uniquely Old South.

She was a woman who left footprints behind that will never be swept away by the winds of time.

Hers was a life well lived.

DADDY'S WORDS OF WISDOM |

Daddy was right of course.

Always cut away from yourself whenever you're handling a knife.

For a few seconds I stared at the blood gushing from the two inch long laceration that I'd just inflicted on my left picker finger before squeezing off the flow and deciding my next move.

I'd been skinning a vine twisted stick that I intended to fashion into a hiking staff when, against Daddy's age old advice, I pulled the blade toward me. It slipped off the wood causing such carnage that I'd have been arrested for a felony if I'd done it to anybody else.

My first thought, after I assessed the damage and decided that the wound probably wouldn't be fatal, was of Daddy looking down of me, chuckling. I expect that he nudged whoever was sitting next to him, Moses maybe, or Noah, perhaps Uncle K.O. pointing Earthward, directly at me.

"That one was always pretty bullheaded."

One trip to the emergency room and eight stitches later, many years after he left for Heaven, Daddy seemed more the astute sage than ever.

He comes to mind often, my old Southern Daddy.

Often when I think of him I'm reminded of the old Mark Twain adage, or some variation of it, about how our dads, who are as clueless as a box of rocks when we're teenagers, become wiser and smarter as we ourselves age.

Mine was no different. Back then I thought he was a quick tempered taskmaster who had no idea what it was like to be young and forward thinking. He was stuck on a dirt farm with dirt farm ideas that I wanted no part of.

That particular era of my foolishness lasted only a few years. It wasn't long before I understood just how perfectly he fit into his surroundings and how restless I felt in mine.

But even when there was strain between us there was one thing I always felt.

Trust.

When I was around eight years old I climbed up one of the huge pecan trees (that's pe, like green pea, and can, like tin can for anyone who lives north of Hephzibah) in our backyard at the old home place. When I started to shimmy back down I panicked and found myself clinging to the trunk twenty feet off the ground. Mama was in the yard and she told me over and over that there was a limb just inches below my feet but I wouldn't let go of the tree until she drove a mile or two out into the field, retrieved my Daddy and had him tell me about the lifesaving branch underneath.

Once I heard his words I was able to easily slide on down into his arms at which point he promptly swatted me on the butt for delaying his plowing.

That was okay. He'd saved the day.

Daddy had a special treatment for the condition that most teenage boys have experienced since time immemorial.

One Friday night during my high school years I stayed out way too late and did all the imprudent things that prompted somebody long ago to coin the phrase "boys will be boys". When I did finally straggle in Mama was waiting and she did forevermore bless me out. I remember thinking that I'd rather have been arrested in town and thrown in the pokey than to be facing her at that moment in time.

"Your father and I will talk to you about this tomorrow," she huffed and went to bed.

When she referred to him as "your father" I knew I was in big trouble.

"Lord, now would be a good time to return," I prayed, silently of course.

The expected tail chewing never happened but by sunrise Daddy had me sitting on a tractor harrowing a hundred acre field, head throbbing, cotton mouthed, nauseous, cussing the older "friend" who provided the Colt 45 malt liquor the night before, wishing the Savior would heed my earlier plea to hasten back down and lift me off that steel beast.

Daddy's treatment wouldn't really cure a hangover but it certainly made me never want to have another one.

He was wise.

So Daddy, if you're somehow seeing these words from beyond the eastern sky, we still have that same old tractor and every time I see it I think of you.

I promise to cut with the blade away from me from now on.

Thanks for the wisdom.

THIS BOY |

I was stunned by the news.

A heart attack? No way! Not him! He's young. He's as healthy as a horse. There must be some mistake.

I hung up the phone and started planning.

I could be there in three hours if traffic was light.

At the same time I began to have flashbacks.

I saw a skinny little towhead Southern boy, no shirt, cut off blue jeans and no shoes.

His weekend playground was Granddaddy's farm and he took full advantage of it. There were trees to climb, woods to explore, endless fields to run and play in. One pond to swim in, another just for fishing. Rides on the old tractor. His energy seemed boundless.

A heart attack? Impossible!

Minutes later I was on the road driving too fast, determined to get there quickly.

The boy and his older sister were my folks first and only grandchildren until my oldest arrived years later. Holding the lofty status of the first granddaughter and first grandson afforded them plenty of doting from the grandparents, aunts and uncles.

I lived far away but had my special times too.

One year I took the two of them to Tybee Island for a day

trip. By that time the boy had developed a mischievous streak. Somewhere on the beach he found some white clay that had washed ashore. He covered his palms with the substance and, without me knowing it, he "painted" two perfect handprints on the back of my black swimming suit, one on each cheek. I didn't know about it until I noticed that everybody who passed us was laughing.

I interrupted my memories and looked at the speedometer. Ninety-two.

Slow down mister!

My mind fast forwarded a few years.

We were out in the woods on the annual New Years Day squirrel hunt, several men and a few kids. By then the boy had reached the Southern Alpha Male stage. Still skinny but now tough talking and smart mouthed.

Somebody spotted a squirrel high in the top of a tree. Another fired and the squirrel fell close to the skinny boy. It was still alive.

"Finish him off son", I said to the boy.

He stood there for a minute looking at the animal. He couldn't do it.

"I ain't gonna shoot the poor little thing", he shouted and headed the other direction.

Well, well, still a tender heart inside that mouthy kid.

A tender heart suddenly sick.

Then there was the time when he was older and had saved up his money and bought a used dirt bike. It was a heap of scrap iron and only ran about half the time. Impatient boys want, and expect, their machines to run ALL the time. One day the boy was not able to get the bike to crank. He had kicked the starter dozens of times with no luck and was beyond frustrated. Being a poor mechanic I was no help and after a while he threw the bike down and let loose with a string of sentences that sounded like the proverbial drunken sailor except for the fact that he didn't utter a single cuss word. He wanted to, I could tell. But out of respect for his old uncle he managed to chew out the hunk of metal without actually swearing. I had to walk away to keep him from seeing me laughing at his misfortune.

" God, reach down. Touch this boy."

I jump forward many years. Now I see the boy standing under an arbor with the sun starting to set in the west. His wedding. He'd finally met his match. A little blond fireball about half his size had stolen his heart.

"Heal his heart Lord"

When I finally got to the hospital I found exactly what I expected. This wonderful Southern family had mobilized. I had to fight my way through a crowd of more than fifty friends and kin. My brothers, the boy's dad and uncle, had taken charge and were directing the family traffic. His mother and aunts were greeting visitors, hugging, supporting.

The little blond fireball was by the boy's side.

I walked in and saw him laying there, a little pale but otherwise alert and chipper. I knew then that he was going to be okay.

"Good thing there was a rain delay cause you're making me miss the race", I said.

He laughed and asked, "Did you drive here from Charleston?"

"Yes I did", I replied.

"Why? I'm fine", he said

"For the same reason you'll drive to Charleston when it's my turn to have a heart attack", I answered.

The boy understood.

That's what families do.

Families, Yours And Mine |

Just admit it, you have relatives.

You have kinfolk.

You weren't hatched, you were born, and by that very fact there has to be at least a few people on the planet who you are kin to, no matter how much you wish it wasn't so.

You can deny it till the bovines make their slow journey back to the homestead, no matter how much they embarrass you or humiliate you, unless you arrived alone from another planet (not totally out of the realm of possibility for some local folks I've encountered) you have a family.

So just suck it up and deal with it.

If you grew up in the South it's even worse.

Personally, if my figures are correct, I'm kin to eighty-three point two percent of the folks in my home county.

It's so bad that, even now, if I'm considering asking a lady out on a date, it requires me to do several hours of genealogical research to determine if she is related to me before I dare make that first phone call. Because if she is kin to me, even if she nor I are aware of it, somebody does know, trust me. And, as soon as she and I are seen out in public together, before you can say Cousin Honey, I'm branded a heathen, her Mama is begging her to be re-baptized and somebody is calling Jerry Springer.

It's a sad and unbendable rule of life that, from the very second you spring forth from your mother's womb, you have zero control over who you're kin to.

Once you're here, it's too late. You're trapped.

And it continues throughout a lifetime with more births and marriages adding to the already burgeoning total. It's not inconceivable, with my huge family, that I could one day end up being related by blood or by marriage to ALL of yall!

It boggles the mind.

I'm kin to so many people around the Blessed South that it requires no less that four family reunions every year to get them all covered.

Going to weddings, and funerals, and housewarmings and baby showers is almost like having a part time job in our clan.

And, with a family that big, there are bound to be more than a few who can mortify you without trying very hard.

But, as Southerners, we were counseled years ago by the great philosopher Lewis Grizzard, to put our crazies right out on the front porch for the world to see. Not to hide them away in a locked room like they do Up North.

Daddy was by no means a snob and, based on the fact that I am still cleaning up some of the junk he piled in the woods ten years after he left us, he wasn't the most orderly farmer ever born either. But I remember him shaking his head in exasperation when we drove by a close relative's house one afternoon and saw a new addition to the place.

"Only he would build a hog pen in his front yard!" Daddy snorted.

I've laughed about it over the years but I have no doubt that Daddy would have defended that same kinsman with physical ardor against anybody else.

After all, even though you can't choose your relatives, they are YOUR relatives.

So, if you visit one of your cousins and you see that he has planted flowers in a couple of discarded toilets, one on each side of the steps to his house, as a matter of Southern etiquette, you just tip your hat and tell him how pretty the flowers are. You don't have to mention the commodes unless he brings them up first.

Another relative decides to dye his hair platinum blond and start wearing women's clothes. You grit your teeth and smile and tell folks a little white lie about him having delayed shell shock syndrome from some long ago foreign conflict. Then you make a mental note to put him on the Sunday School prayer list at the earliest opportunity.

You have a relative who is renowned for gardening naked. You caution him to use extra sun screen on the more tender parts and warn your daughters and nieces to never drop by his house without calling first.

What you never, ever do is deny kinship.

Never.

That would be a very UnSouthern thing to do.

In my family, whether you land there by birth, marriage or adoption, you're there for life.

There's no escape.

For better or for worse, I'll take my family over any other. Quirks, idiosyncrasies and eccentricities notwithstanding.

You know exactly what I mean. Because you have a family too. Just admit it.

From Southland To Glory Land |

It was a quiet conversation, whispered because of where we were.

The talk was bittersweet, but the words were sincere and necessary, at least for me.

The exchange was really no exchange at all. The talk was very one sided.

I spoke softly to my granddaughter, the youngest, the newest life in our little sub-clan who lay sleeping peacefully in my arms, oblivious to what was happening. Down the hall her great grandmother, the one I call Mama, was also sleeping, mostly peacefully.

The baby's mother, my middle child, and my two other kids were with other members of the family surrounding Mama, telling her that they loved her and how thankful they were to have her in their lives. I got to stay with The Princess. No children were allowed on the hall where Mama lay, hopefully hearing those words of adoration from her extended brood, hopefully feeling the gentle touches, the kisses to her forehead.

Children were not allowed where Mama lay dying. So I got to hold the sweet baby girl for a while, just us two.

I told her all about Mama.

Of course she won't remember our little talk. She's only a year old, but there will be other talks, stories, remembrances. She won't have any memory of Mama but she will know her, know who she was, what she meant to our family.

She'll know. I'll make certain of that.

She'll hear how Mama draped me, already fully grown at 14 years old, over her shoulder and half carried me in and out of hospitals and doctors offices as I recovered from a ruptured appendix, she herself not yet healed from her own major surgery.

She'll know that Mama once made the best biscuits ever baked anywhere in the universe, two full pans every morning, right up until the day she discovered the instant canned ones.

I'll tell her the story about Mama killing a nasty old rat and how she then paid homage to it with her tears.

My granddaughter will know that Mama patched up and salved and bandaged a million of my cuts, scrapes and bruises when I was a child and did her best to help me mend a broken heart or two along the way.

She'll see a precious picture taken during her first year of life and Mama's last, sitting with the three other great-grands, all girls, with Mama in the middle.

I would have taken a lot more pictures if I'd known there'd be no more opportunities.

If only.

But it's okay because in our world, words are just as important as photographs and that's what I will give my grandbaby and any others that come after her.

Words about Mama.

She'll know all about a woman that she will never see because that's what we do in my family.

Nobody is ever really and truly gone as long as there are stories to tell and re-tell and tell again.

Two days after my first talk with the little one about her great grandmother, Mama died.

In the twinkling of an eye she traveled from the rural roads of Dixieland to a street of gold in Beulah Land.

So we're orphans now, SherryLou, Willie, Urb and me since Mama flew away. But we're only orphans in the earthly sense because she and Daddy taught us from our births till their deaths how to be His children. They staked us to a legacy on both sides of our Southern lineage rooted deeply in the belief that this life is simply a stepping stone to the next, much greater one.

In her twilight years Mama didn't talk much, mostly she just sat and listened. I often couldn't tell whether she had any idea what was being said around her or if she even knew who some of us were.

But then, during a Wednesday or Sunday night church service, she would be called on to pray. The clarity instantly returned and there was no doubt that she knew exactly Who she was talking to.

She knew what was really important and, hopefully, she gave a bit of that knowledge to me.

That day at the hospital as I gazed at my sleeping granddaughter, I wondered aloud.

"What will you do, who will you become, what will you accomplish in the next eight decades till you're as old as Mama?"

Of course there's no way to know the answers but what I am certain of is that she's been gifted with a great start, a magnificent legacy, in large part because of who her great-grandmother was, and is.

Thank you Mama. From the Princess. From me.

From all of us.

III

UNCLE ENOCH

*"He's a walking contradiction,
partly truth and partly fiction."*

~ Kris Kristofferson ~

Uncle Enoch And The Cannon |

There sits, on the lawn of the courthouse in Athens, Georgia, a reminder that a fine concept can be a poor reality.

The world's only double barreled cannon.

Built in 1862 during the Civil War, it looks impressive.

Looks can be deceiving.

It was supposed to simultaneously fire two cannonballs linked by a chain. The balls would stretch the chain between the two as they roared forward theoretically "mowing down" the enemy.

It was a great idea except for one problem.

It didn't work.

When the cannon was test fired in Athens the two fuses did not burn at the same speed. One side fired a split second before the other causing the balls to spin out of control doing more damage to crops, livestock and buildings than to the test targets.

After the failure of the weapon in Athens, it was shipped to Augusta for further testing.

There were those who believed that the cannon could be tinkered with and perfected.

It was tested by the military at the Augusta Arsenal and again failed miserably.

It would seem after two unsuccessful experiments with the gun that it would have been abandoned or discarded but that's not what happened.

While the above accounts are historically documented, there is a little known and rarely reported footnote to the story of the double barreled cannon.

That's where my Uncle Enoch enters the historical record.

The weapon somehow drew the attention of a newly arrived group of men who claimed to be investors. They were mostly strangers to the locals, and they held an overly enthusiastic interest in the cannon. They were granted permission to test the weapon, however, after much discussion over its reliability, none of the strangers wanted to be the one to light the fuses and risk lasting humiliation or injury.

Uncle Enoch was my great, great uncle. My family reveres our ancestors but for some reason Uncle Enoch is rarely mentioned.

He was, however, well known locally back then so when the strangers inquired as to someone who might be willing to ignite the fuses, Uncle Enoch was the nearly unanimous suggestion.

A group was dispatched to the local saloons to search him out and, sure enough, he was promptly located. He was reluctant to leave but was persuaded after being told that he would be driven back to the same spot and paid appropriately, if he fired the cannon successfully. With that promise he gulped his last few drams and hurriedly left the establishment with the strangers.

The long ride back was over rutted mud streets. Uncle Enoch immediately realized that he had neglected nature's call before boarding the wagon, but, for once in his life he was being given real responsibility and he intended to carry out the mission without complaint.

When he arrived at the firing spot Uncle Enoch was handed two burning torches as soon as he alit the buckboard. Though growing more uncomfortable by the minute, he enjoyed the attention.

Then the discussions began. The strangers argued over fuse length, shot sizes, whether to shoot over the Savannah River or into a nearby pine thicket, anything that could be disputed. Meanwhile, the afternoons previously consumed whiskey was making Uncle Enoch extremely fidgety.

Finally, the moment of truth arrived. The men gathered behind the cannon and somebody motioned for Uncle Enoch to light the fuses, but by then he was in agony, literally dancing from one foot to the other. So as not to embarrass himself, when he could wait not another second, he handed the igniters to one of the strangers and sprinted for the woods.

An impatient fellow, the man to whom the torches were passed immediately touched each fuse.

Apparently, one of them was damp and did not light. When the dry side fired, that ball roared from the gun while the second ball stayed firmly in place.

The first shot, linked to the second by the chain swung around behind the cannon and sent the entire group of strangers to their just rewards.

Uncle Enoch was the only survivor.

It was later learned that the strangers were northern spies in the area to steal technology, so, there was not much local mourning.

Years later, in his memoirs, Uncle Enoch wrote, " Had I not stepped away when I did, I would have spent eternity with a full bladder and the full knowledge that I was just as stone dumb as that bunch of Yankee boys". He added, "I never understood why nary a one of them had the good sense to duck"

Uncle Enoch lived 107 years and never married or had children.

That's the historical tale as I know it.

Uncle Enoch's Near Miss |

The year was 1864.

My great Uncle Enoch, who was the only survivor of the test firing of the infamous double barreled cannon early in the Civil War, was 29 years old. He hadn't initially been pressed into service in the Confederate army because he had a foot problem.

Enoch had the same number of toes as everybody else. The problem was, he was born with seven on his left foot and only three on his right. He tended to walk in circles a lot and that wreaked havoc in the ranks when the army was attempting to march in formation.

So Enoch was politely rejected for service.

However, by 1864, there was a much greater need for able bodied men to serve the South. By that point able bodied had taken on a new definition and basically meant that the soldier could stand erect and fire a weapon semi accurately.

So, Enoch joined up.

Other than his tendency to overindulge in the spirits, and his lack of digits on one foot and the overabundance of them on the other, he was a decent soldier. He didn't eat much and he wasn't smart enough to know that he was supposed to complain about the conditions.

And he was a good shot. He had knocked many a squirrel from the top of the massive cypress trees in the Georgia swamps and he could hit a rabbit on the run with his rickety old musket.

When he finally entered the army late in 1863 he was issued a used Sharps carbine by the quartermaster and was told that the weapon had been in constant use by one army or the other since the beginning of the conflict.

All of its previous users had apparently met their Maker.

During his first two years in the army Enoch was assigned to several different companies. It wasn't planned that way. It was due to his marching problem. He often got lost and because of his foot affliction he would just continue walking in huge circles until he met up with other Southern soldiers.

In early December of 1864 Enoch found himself attached to the company commanded by General Joseph "Fightin' Joe" Wheeler, the Army of Tennessee.

One cold night Enoch ran into his distant cousin Hezekiah.

"Well Hezzie. Ain't seen you in a while", said Enoch.

"Nope, been a coon's age I reckon," replied Hezekiah.

With the re-acquaintance business out of the way the boys began to ramble around the encampment in search of a strong drink.

They soon located a small group passing around a jug of some sort of potato liquor concoction. It had a horrible taste but produced the desired results quickly.

All the talk was of the impending arrival of General William T. Sherman and his pillagers. Word was that the Northern army was within hours of reaching the area.

The soldiers began to brag about their marksmanship and each was sure that he'd shoot Willie T. at his first appearance.

"I seen Enoch shoot a buzzard out of the sky half a mile up", said Hezekiah.

"Well if Sherman bothers to show up around here maybe Enoch can shoot another buzzard," snorted a tipsy corporal.

It turns out Enoch got his chance.

On December 4th the Northern army attacked and the fighting was fierce. It was a back and forth battle with the Southerners gaining the advantage only to be repelled by the North. The boys in blue would push forward but would be driven back by Wheeler's men.

Suddenly, amid the smoke and dust of the fighting appeared none other than William Sherman himself astride a fine horse.

They all knew immediately who it was. They'd seen his pictures in newspapers for years.

Uncle Enoch was about fifty yards from Sherman and decided it was now or never. He was still feeling the effects of the potato mash and his head was spinning but he knew that he could make the shot.

He took careful aim. Held his breath. Squeezed the trigger.

And hiccupped.

The shot went low and killed the general's horse. His aides quickly hustled him away and he was not seen again.

Years later Uncle Enoch's memoirs read as follows:

" My shot flew low and I hit the horse instead of the horse's ass named Sherman".

Down through history many claimed to be the confederate who shot Sherman's horse from under him near Waynesboro in 1864 but this tale should put all the others to rest.

It was Uncle Enoch.

Uncle Enoch In The Lion's Den |

You might remember my great Uncle Enoch. He was the only survivor of a test firing of the infamous double barreled cannon in the early years of the Civil War and later shot a horse out from under General Sherman during the battle of Waynesboro in 1864.

Uncle Enoch lived a long and colorful 107 years.

He had seven toes on his left foot and only three on his right. During his stint in the army his digital imbalance manifested itself in his inability to traverse terrain in a straight line.

After the war Enoch, having been granted a small Confederate pension, bought a few acres of land and a mule of disagreeable temperament. He had never farmed so his neighbors quietly questioned the wisdom of his agricultural endeavors.

Their doubts were well founded.

One day Enoch was attempting to convince the ornery animal to pull a plow when the mule suddenly flung his back end into the air and attempted to kick Enoch. He managed to dodge the assault but when the mule came down one of it's hooves landed directly on top of his left foot instantly severing three of the seven toes.

It was weeks before Enoch was able to walk but when he did, with only four toes remaining on his left foot and the original three on his right, he was, for the first time in his life, able to walk somewhat normally.

He deemed the incident to be miracle and in his thankfulness immediately vowed to give up liquor.

Unfortunately, quitting alcohol didn't make him any less unintelligent.

Enoch was not a ladies man, but, having gained a bit of wartime notoriety, he was not totally devoid of female companionship.

One year he met a woman named Annie when he was in Savannah with some of his kinsmen. They had walked to the coast to bring back salt and coffee.

She was up from the Everglades of Florida, rough as an armadillo's backside and meaner than a copperhead. She wore overalls and brogan boots. She'd brought a load of alligator meat to Savannah to be sold in the markets.

For reasons known only to God, Enoch was smitten.

He immediately asked the woman if she would allow him to court her.

"You can if you can find your way to my swamp," she grunted around a wad of tobacco in her jaw, then added, " I'm a lady. Don't bring your sorry self without a gift in hand."

As soon as possible Enoch set out for Florida. He made it all the way to Annie's home without incident. When he spotted her shanty on the edge of the glades he paused to take in the sight. There she sat in a cane bottomed chair on the porch, corn cob pipe clenched in her teeth, skinning a possum.

Suddenly he remembered that he'd forgotten to bring a gift. He began to panic but before he could ponder the problem, out of nowhere he was attacked by a Florida black panther.

He fought with all his might against the whirlwind of claws and teeth. One minute the panther had the upper hand, then Enoch gained control and pinned the animal to the ground. The animal wriggled free and the fight was on again.

For what must have felt like forty days and forty nights Enoch and the panther battled while Annie just sat and watched. The struggle rolled into Annie's yard where he was finally able to grab a horsehair rope and hogtie the beast.

Struggling for air and lying flat on his back Enoch looked up to see Annie smiling down at him.

"I wish you'd brung me a dog. I ain't partial to cats," she said. "But, it is a thoughty gift so I reckon we can commence proper courtin' and sparkin' now."

"Another miracle," Enoch thought. He immediately swore to quit cussing.

Annie set about patching up Enoch's wounds and thus began an improbable relationship that lasted many years.

She kept the panther. He gave it a wide berth.

When Enoch returned to Georgia the clan gathered around to hear all about his trip.

Not the least bit gifted in conversational skills he answered most of the inquiries with a muttered "yup" or "nah". But then one of the ladies asked him what Annie looked liked.

Enoch beamed as if picturing his beloved.

"Well, she ain't all that ugly and some of her teeth ain't quit her yet."

Romantic attraction. Who can explain it?

Enoch continued to travel to Florida to see Annie and never again had to fight any wild creatures to win her affection.

That's the true tale as I know it.

Uncle Enoch And The Mighty Wind |

Nobody really knows exactly how my great, great Uncle Enoch ended up on a cattle ranch Out West, but he did.

A few years after he'd lost three of the seven toes on his left foot when a mule stepped on him, inspiring him to give up hard drink, Enoch found that his life was much less difficult when he was able to occasionally sneak a few hits from whatever bottle of spirits happened to appear near him.

So, as with most mortals, he sometimes forgot his vow.

Consequently, every once in a while, his on-again, off-again Everglades swamp gal, Annie, would run him off and dare him to ever come back.

So, even though he and Annie courted until he was over a hundred years old, Enoch continued to find misadventures everywhere he ventured, quite often accompanied by his distant cousin Hezekiah.

Though many of the facts about Uncle Enoch have been lost to history, the legendary tales indicate that he was at the center, or at least around the edges, of many occurrences that are well known and well documented. Such as the pivotal part he played in the test firing of the infamous double barreled cannon and his presence at the Civil War battle where he shot a horse out from under General William Sherman.

He was also reputed to have been a part of the burial detail after the Battle of Little Bighorn, also known as Custer's Last Stand.

That may explain how, in the autumn of 1876, Enoch and Hezekiah found themselves in the employ of Mr. Charlie Goodnight, one time frontiersman and Texas Ranger, and by then owner of the largest cattle ranch in America.

The boys endured some ribbing from the more experienced cowhands due to the fact that neither of them was particularly rapid on the uptick, and it didn't help that both were still wearing the old Brogan army boots from their soldiering days, with their spurs tied on with rawhide strips.

Nevertheless, Enoch and Hezzie became good riders and ropers and spent much of their time rounding up the wild cattle all over the Goodnight ranch. They worked as partners and were away from the ranch for weeks at a time locating and herding the feral cows into makeshift pens throughout the Palo Dura Canyon in the Texas panhandle.

One afternoon when the two cousins had gotten tired of eating their own cooking they decided to strike out for the ranch, about thirty miles away. They got there just as the dinner bell was ringing.

Old Charlie Goodnight himself came out to greet the boys and invited them to come eat in the big house. After weeks out on the range they were unaccustomed to indoor dining so they politely declined. Mr. Goodnight understood so he gave the boys a bottle of tequila and told the cook to see that they were properly fed out by the fire.

They had ridden hard and had jumped plenty of gullies and creeks so their innards were a bit shook up, but they were also famished so they went through several helpings of frijoles and beefsteak. They also polished off the half gallon of tequila in quick fashion. Then they laid back against their bedrolls to let the food settle.

And settle it did.

Uncle Enoch began to feel more than a little gaseous, like his belly was ready to explode. So he did what cowboys have done for eons.

He lifted his leg just a little and cut loose with the loudest breakage of intestinal wind that any human ever witnessed.

It was a historic effort.

The mesquite trees swayed.

Coyotes off in the distance went silent in mid howl.

The horses in the corral got very quiet.

The flames on the fire actually moved.

Enoch just grinned at Hezzie and Hezzie grinned back.

Until they looked up and saw the beautiful Mexican girl who had brought them their supper standing there with a pan of biscuits in her hands and a puzzled look on her face.

Enoch was mortified.

" Lord help me, Hezzie! She heard that!" He wanted to crawl under his horse and hide.

" So what?" Hezzie replied, unconcerned.

" I'm mightily embarrassed! That's so what!"

" Ain't no need for that." Hezzie said.

" And why not?"

" Cause, I happen to know, she don't know no English." Hezzie announced confidently.

" You shore about that?" asked Enoch hopefully.

" Yep. She don't speak it and she don't understand it neither."

That settled that.

Both of them, mollified by their sincere belief that even flatulence had to be spoken and comprehended in one's own language, dropped off to sleep in their bedrolls under the vast Texas sky.

Somewhere off in the distance the coyotes resumed their night songs.

IV

THE BLESSED SOUTH

"If you're born in the South,
even if you are moved away as a child,
you carry with you some innate ability
to always be southern.
You never really leave the South.
The South is part of your being."

D.C.L.

"I can't pronounce my R's and G's,
when I'm speakin' Southernese."

~ Jimmy Buffett ~

Random Ruminations |

Dixie.

What a perfectly fine geographical nickname!

Think about it. What other area of the country has it's very own nickname that, regardless of where you travel, is synonymous with that area.

Where everybody knows your name.

Of course, not only is the name unique.

Dixie, my homeland and maybe yours, is unique.

I often ponder on my motivations for coming back home to the Blessed South after being away for so many years.

Here, in no particular order and for no other reason than I took a notion to list them, is a cornucopia of unsystematic ramblings.

Isn't it fine to live in a place where you can still buy a cane pole. Get yourself one of the long bamboo rods, a bucket of crickets or a box of red wigglers and you'll spend a day snatching redbreasts or bluegills out of a pond somewhere.

What could be better.

Where else in America do magnolia trees thrive. Those magnificently fragrant creations supposedly grow in other areas of the nation but I've never seen any north of the Mason-Dixon line. I don't blame them. Why would they want to put down roots anywhere else? Around these parts you will see magnolias adorning the grounds of the finest mansions and also still holding forth at ancient home sites where the buildings and barns were long ago reclaimed by the soil.

Magnolias may just be God's finest Southern artwork.

Around these parts you can still find churches where you are not required to "try out" in order to sing in the choir. You don't even have to know how to sing. I'm living proof. All you need is a desire to make a joyful noise, a willingness to show up for practice and a smiling face. You'll more than likely be surrounded by folks who DO know how to make music with their voices and nobody will notice that you couldn't carry a tune in a croker sack.

Did you know that there are places in America where you can't park your own pick up truck in your own driveway? It's hard to believe but it's true. Codes in certain neighborhoods prevent what they term as "eyesores" from assaulting the sensibilities of the more upper crust residents.

What a crock!

Can you imagine a neighborhood where it's illegal to park a BMW or a Mercedes? Where only Silverados and F150s are allowed?

I'm all for restrained code enforcement, but Down South a man's ride is as much a part of his castle as the Lazy Boy.

I'm glad that I reside among more sagacious Southern folk.

It makes me happy that I live in a region where I only need to speak one language.

Southernese.

Granted, depending on what part of Dixie you find yourself in, the length of the drawn out drawls and the regional dialects may require you to lean in closer and concentrate a little harder to understand what's being mumbled at you, but Southerners can communicate among themselves just fine thank you.

Fried green tomatoes is a Southland delicacy, not just a chick flick movie. Any vegetable can and will be fried down here. Squash. Okra. Corn. Dill pickles. Okay, they were cucumbers before they were pickles but the you see my point.

It's terrific to live where there are four distinct seasons.

Fall. Winter. Spring.

And Summer, otherwise known as Ten Degrees Hotter Than Unshaded Hades.

If you don't want to you don't have to change your wardrobe all that much from season to season except for a few minor adjustments. Starting in late April you can quit wearing socks and long pants for several months except of course when you might find yourself in the choir singing poorly. You don't want to call any more attention to yourself then your bellowing baritone already does. Even when winter does finally arrive, most days a light jacket will keep you snug. Down South you can wear Hawaiian shirts, no matter how outlandish, during any season. And most folks won't even notice if you wear white after Labor Day.

Four seasons indeed.

In our part of the universe you can eat breakfast in Jacksonville, dinner in Savannah and supper in Charleston, never break the speed limit and never be more than a pebbles fling from the ocean. (if you happen to be a visiting Yankee, that's breakfast, lunch and dinner, but if you're a visiting Yankee you probably missed the point of all this anyway)

Just a few of my Southern musings. There are plenty more where those came from.

Down here in Dixie.

My Young South |

The Old South.

Depending on who's pontificating, the term Old South is either revered or reviled.

Not much middle ground.

Even though the true Old South was gone with the wind decades before Daddy and Mama were twinkles in the eyes of Grandma Julia and Grandma Freddie respectively, I can understand why there are differing opinions about life in our homeland as it was all those years ago.

No era in any part of history, in any part of the world, is without it's share of glory and of shame.

But by the time I made my grand entrance into Dixieland, the South was an easy paced, uncomplicated place to be a dirt farm boy.

I'm certain that some will disagree, but to me, a barefoot kid ignorant of and unconcerned about politics and world affairs, the South was the smack dab center of the universe.

Later in life I contracted a deadly case of wanderlust that I still suffer from today. But as a youngster a few thousand country acres and perhaps a weekly trip to the one screen picture show in town was all I needed to be content.

Life in my neck of the woods was interesting. Sometimes fun, sometimes eccentric.

Never boring.

I skipped kindergarten, we lived too far out in the country, but I got a fine start on my education by listening to men telling stories, some true, some not so much, while sitting on upturned Coca Cola crates at Mister Scott's store. The men seemed old and wise but in reality were probably considerably younger than I am now. I learned many lessons sitting at the feet of those fellows on that hard wood plank floor.

That was my South.

My knowledge of other parts of the world began in bed late at night when I would hide under the covers and listen to faraway radio stations on my transistor radio. WBT in Charlotte. WLS in Chicago. WOWO in Fort Wayne, Indiana.

And my favorite, WWL, " way down yonder on New Orleans". The bayou accents of the deejays on that powerhouse channel sounded just as foreign, though not nearly as harsh, as the Northern parlance I heard from Yankee acquaintances.

Those stations could be heard all over the South and in many parts of America until the government decided that there was something unfair about that.

These days I can't pick up AM stations that are thirty miles away.

The South of my youth was roamed by root doctors, rock doctors, mineral doctors, and all other manner of hucksters plying their supposedly medicinal wares. And for every peddler trying to convince his customers that a hunk of limestone could cure rheumatism there were plenty of folks, some of them my kin, willing to hand over their sawmill dollars to give it a try.

In rural Southern America back then there were fewer teeth. Fewer real ones anyway. I was often amused at some of my older relatives who, once their few remaining teeth surrendered, tried dentures for a while only to decide that they were too much trouble and that a good set of gums was all that was required to eat most Southern food anyway.

Thank the Lord for the fluoride introduction to the drinking water back then. My generation is much too vain to walk around toothless.

We had a grand total of three TV stations, all part time and all black and white. Locally produced shows kept me rapt for hours. Sheriff John enforcing the law and hosting a kids show at the same time Trooper Terry was fighting bad guys on another station. Bwana John leading expeditions into darkest Africa with a Georgia accent and silly turtle shell hat. Sometimes Mama would have to make me go out to play if the "fuss box", Daddy's epithet for the RCA, was too addicting.

Today I have five hundred channels and sometimes go for days without switching on the set.

To be sure, my young South was a different place.

It was a world where you could leave a dime in the mailbox on top of an unstamped letter. Later you'd find your change, two pennies, in the mailbox and the letter on the way to it's destination.

Where clothes were hung on lines in backyards to dry. The smell of clean sheets softened by the sun and the Southern breezes will never be duplicated by anything found in a bottle of Downy.

Where we put peanuts in our Cokes long before Tim McGraw, who by the way I doubt ever actually consumed the crunchy delicacy, sang about it.

A different world, yes, but today's South ain't bad either.

I like it here.

I'm staying.

KEEPING IT SIMPLE DOWN SOUTH |

I've noticed that modern society seems to like to make things more difficult than necessary.

We all know that the computer age has been here for a while and it's not going away, and most of us have found a fairly comfortable spot within that complicated world and are doing okay in spite of having not the foggiest notion what a gigabyte is or knowing the difference between a hard drive and a driveshaft.

Computers even come with their own languages, though I am not familiar with a single human being that can adequately explain to me what that means.

According to Wikipedia, computer languages can be used to, among other things, express algorithms precisely.

Algorithms?

Be honest. Before you reached for the Webster's, where you didn't find that word and subsequently had to Google it, did you have a clue as to what it meant?

Me either.

Communication, spoken, written, or barfed out by a computer is one thing, but our true language, the kind that comes out of your mouth, not your Hewlett Packard, has also become more difficult to speak and to comprehend.

How did this happen? When did we get to be so sensitive that certain words which were perfectly fine for centuries have now become offensive?

Heavy folks are now referred to as obese or weight challenged.

Stuttering folks don't stutter, they have speech impediments.

We've even had to start calling short people by a more politically correct name. Vertically challenged. Heaven forbid that we refer to anyone as a midget or dwarf, even though both of those are entirely good words that have appeared in every dictionary ever printed with the simple definition being "an extremely small person". What's distasteful about that?

I made the mistake of using the word midget once and was quickly and pointedly corrected by my friend.

" Those folks now prefer to be called Little People," she sniffed.

" We already have a group designated as little people," I corrected back. " They're called children."

She wasn't amused.

Down South, folks have a fine way of cutting right to the chase when using the local language.

Here are a few examples.

The Yankee version of an old saying.

" Providing that the Benevolent Supreme Being is disposed to allow an encounter and on the condition that the small, meandering body of water does not reach a level higher than it's earthen banks provides for, we shall catch sight of the sum total of you when this day is gone and the next one has begun."

The Dixie version.

" See yall tomorrow if the Good Lord's willing and the creek don't rise."

A phrase that you might hear anywhere north of the Mason-Dixon line.

" He has been affected by his excessive intake of copious amounts of intoxicating beverages to such an extent that he has taken on the persona of a small, playful jungle primate."

Down here in Dixie we have a much more concise way of saying the same thing and getting the point across even better.

" He's drunk as a monkey."

A Northern description of aggressive behavior.

" Approximating and similar to the actions taken by a large

passerine bird that forms the genus Corvus in the family Cordidae, when said bird is in the process of attacking and consuming a Cotinis nitida."

The Southern translation.

" Like a crow on a June bug"

An implied threat by some of our Northern friends.

" Male human who has not yet reached manhood! Utilizing an unclenched fist I shall strike you with such force that you will be temporarily rendered mentally incapacitated!"

Convert that snotty phrase to good old down home Southernese and you get this.

" Boy! I'll slap you silly!"

A weather prognostication from parts other than these.

" Conditions are such that the firmament is about to open up and water will cascade downward in such torrents that it will appear as if felines and canines are tumbling from the clouds"

The interpretation from around here.

" It's fixin' to rain cats and dogs."

You get the picture.

Even though the tall tale telling in my family often requires that we abstain from using one word when ten words would be more colorful, in most cases, like these I've described, nothing beats good old Southern succinctness.

And now, due to my recent lack of voluntary unconsciousness I have reached a level of fatigue that requires me to retire to my sleeping quarters. I bid you a most pleasant evening.

Nah. How about this.

I'm whipped and hittin' the hay.

Night, yall.

Movin' Slow |

Daddy had a two word phrase that he often used to describe any of his sons or other indentured servants moving slower than he thought that the task at hand required.

Half assing.

If you grew up in the South you know exactly what it means.

I think he had it wrong though. I'm not convinced that the slower pace was intentional or for lack of desire to do a good job.

I suspect it was more a matter of doing what most Southerners are bred to do.

Mosey.

I never tried to work slow just to irritate Daddy.

I was just moseyin'.

Technically, it should be spelled moseying, but adding the g to the pronunciation makes it sound like a Yankee word that no child of the South worth his sassafras would ever utter.

Mosey.

It actually is a word, not just a colloquialism.

Mosey / (mozee) verb. To walk in a leisurely manner. Oxford American Dictionary.

People outside of the South attempt to use the word but it just doesn't seem to work for them.

A cop buddy who was born and raised in Boston would often say " Okay boys, I have to mosey", whenever break was over and he'd have to get back on the street. Then he'd tear out of the parking lot like his badge was on fire.

I'd hardly call that moseyin'.

I offered to demonstrate to the younger officers the true art of going from point a to point b, with genuine determination and purpose but in a much more relaxed mode. They all declined preferring to be in a perpetual hurry.

That's beyond my comprehension.

What's the big rush?

Truthfully though, there's no real way to describe moseyin' but Southerners instinctively recognize it when we see it.

Growing up I knew a man, known only as Big Boy, who walked everywhere he went. I never saw him in a car. Even when I would occasionally stop and offer him a ride, he'd refuse. He weighed over four hundred pounds so it's possible that he couldn't fit in most cars but, regardless, he had moseyin' down to a science.

He would often walk from his house to the old store near our homeplace, not more than three miles, but he would turn it into an all day event.

Once when we were pulling weeds in a field near the store and the highway we saw him coming and out of boredom we timed how long it took him to cover the quarter mile as compared to how many rows we ridded of Johnson grass and other insidious plant life.

It wasn't even close. We nearly finished the field.

The fellow knew how to mosey.

I had an uncle, long passed on, who was an accomplished moseyer. He never seemed to be overly anxious to get anywhere. He often went barefoot even when he walked in the woods. His particular method of doing the mosey involved knowing exactly where and when, and how slowly, to put his foot down. He'd amble around for hours, hands deep in his pockets, which by the way is a characteristic common to most moseyers, and never get a scratch.

Incidentally, it's possible to mosey while sitting behind a steering wheel. Ever been behind a driver with the left elbow hanging out the window, driving fifteen miles below the speed limit, blinker on for a half mile before the simple right turn into the driveway that requires both lanes and five minutes to accomplish?

Sure you have.

That's what I call motor moseyin'.

Daddy, the same gent who would often harangue me about moving slow, once inadvertently bragged on me for doing exactly that.

We were at the store waiting out a short rain when I heard him comparing me to my brothers while talking to the other farmers.

"If a snake or a rabbit crossed the field that boy (me) will see the track. He finds arrowheads on the ground that the others stepped over. He notices everything".

Actually, thinking back on it, I honestly don't know if he was bragging or lamenting but what he described was classic moseyin'.

I can proudly proclaim, after a lifetime of practicing the craft, that I still know how.

Quite simply, nature didn't equip me with the physiology required for rapid motion. Why pretend to want to be in a hurry when it's so alien to me?

I just don't want to miss anything.

Anyway, enough for now.

Time to mosey.

Our Small Town |

When I moved back to the homeplace, after living away for so many years, I often remembered of the old saying, " The more things change, the more they stay the same".

So true of my hometown.

Recently, on a Tuesday, I spent nearly all day in town. Normally, I spend most of my time at my place out in the country.

But that day I had several errands in town so I decided to make a day of it.

I started the day by dropping off my truck to have new tires put on. I took it to a business that has been around since before I was born. I've known the family who owns it all of my life. My brother married into that family and is a manager at the business.

Since it was going to take a while to get the truck serviced I decided to take the short walk downtown and have lunch. I went to a popular café where I had never eaten before. The food was great, the service was perfect and as I ate I thought back to the times I had been in the same building.

Years ago it was known as The Record Rack. It was run by Mrs. Watson who sold 45 rpm's and LP albums. I remember when she removed all of the Beatles records from her store after John Lennon made his famous statement about the group being more popular than Jesus Christ.

She never again sold music by the most popular band of all time, and I'm sure she lost a lot of money for her decision.

That was standing on principle.

After a fine lunch I took a stroll through the downtown area.

I stopped for a minute in front of where the hardware store once was. The building stands empty now but I remembered when Daddy bought my first shotgun there. Another family I've known forever owned the business. Years before, when they were in high school, Daddy and the owner of the store played football side by side. Decades later I played football side by side with his son. Same team, same school. We're still friends.

As I passed by the courthouse I stopped at the memorial to the men from the county who have died in foreign wars. On the Viet Nam side I saw several names that I remembered. One who coached me in Midget football. Another who threatened to beat me up at Teen Town. Still another who I remember as a very quiet boy who went to church out in the country with us.

Gone, but I'm certain they aren't forgotten. Not in this small town.

After I picked up my truck I still had a couple of hours before I had a haircut appointment so I headed back out to the country. As I drove I saw a mail truck making the rounds. It was my other brother.

As I passed by a different hardware store I glanced over and saw my cousin who works there. He waved. I waved. Good grief! Is everybody in this town kin to me?

On the way home I drove by our "old" home place, a one hundred acre tract. It was recently sold to a new owner but had once been owned by another of my high school friends. He's been a successful farmer and was elected to the county commission.

Later, back in town, I sat in the barber chair. Behind me, snipping away, was yet another relative. I remembered back to a family reunion when dozens of kids were swimming in the pond.

This cousin was quite young then and somehow got into water over her head and was being drawn toward the spillway. I grabbed her just before she got sucked into the pipe and she still reminds me that I once saved her life.

Just doing my job ma'am.

So, after living away for over half of my life, being back here I see that very little of what is really important has changed. New businesses have come to town. Old businesses, like the downtown hardware store, have faded into history. Politics and demographics have changed. The drug store, with it's lunch counter where we used to hang out, is now a fitness center.

But the important part, the people, remain pretty much the same, and they're still here.

That's a good thing and it suits me just fine.

Small towns, yours and mine. You gotta love them.

Cause some things never change.

LADY LESSONS |

I could have watched them all night.

They were the only ones on the dance floor but neither one seemed at all bothered by that.

They were in their own little world.

Both were barefoot on the cool grass underneath the canopy where the band was playing a blend of country rock and beach music. Both bore radiant smiles. Both wore tee shirts that evidenced their Southern roots.

The love between them was as obvious as the balmy breeze that wafted over the lawn.

And they danced.

They were not some starry-eyed couple. They were much more.

A young mother of the South and her two year old baby girl.

The mom, somewhere in her early twenties, twirled and whirled and boogied the child in endless circles in front of the bandstand and I could hear the baby's gleeful laughter over the rowdy music.

What a perfect picture of Springtime in Dixie.

I began to muse as I watched them dance.

I wished that I was able to film them and capture the special bond between them that's in it's very earliest stages. I'd somehow like to preserve that film and see that the child gets it forty of fifty years from now when her mother is old and tired and no longer able to dance with the same energy.

Between now and then that child may herself grow up to be a Southern mama and, if she could look back and see what I saw that night, she'd be proud of where she came from.

There is something very special about Southern women and, in all my decades of living, I've learned just enough about the species to remain perpetually confused and bewildered.

And enchanted.

I do know a few things about the women of the Blessed South.

Did you know that they are trained from the day they arrive on Earth to speak without uttering a sound?

It's true. Ask any Southern man.

The "looks" that women down here "speak" with run the gamut.

With a demure smile and a gentle fluttering of the eyelashes she can convince a man to do pretty much anything.

Rub her shoulders.

Bring her a pillow.

Repaint the entire house by Friday afternoon when her Mama and Daddy arrive from Charleston.

It's powerful.

On the other end of that scale, Southern women possess a patented look that can send most men cowering.

The stare.

It's withering.

Try to avoid direct eye contact.

If you don't, it'll feel like you've been tomahawked in the solar plexus.

Give a Southern woman an hour to be ready and she will emerge looking like the hottest Broadway model even if she's on a Wal-Mart budget. Whether it's for a high school prom, an evening harbor cruise or simply a night on the town, the ladies around these parts know how to look good.

Real good.

I've learned that Southern women keep food and fixings in the pantry to be used only in the event of a death.

That's right, funeral food, so you best leave it alone.

"You put that right back where you found it. I might need it soon. Old Brother Smith wasn't looking too well at church on Sunday."

A Southern cook can whip up a casserole and have it at the home of the bereaved even before the preacher gets the call.

Speaking of cooking, every Southern lady I know thinks I'll like her sweet potato recipe.

"No thank you ma'am, I don't like sweet potatoes."

"Well, you'll like mine." There's that demure smile.

"But you don't understand, I really hate sweet potatoes."

" Well, Sugar, that's because you haven't tasted mine yet." The smile is tighter now, and a tad edgy.

"Sorry, but I'm not going to eat that."

Oh mercy! The stare!

"On second thought, spoon me up a plateful!"

Yum.

Most of the time, in dealing with a Southern woman, it's best to just nod and agree.

And eat what she serves.

That young mother will no doubt teach her baby girl all of these and many other rules for Southern ladies.

Like it's never too late to send a thank you note.

Or, it's not gossip if it's true.

That Southern men are necessary for the continuation of the population, but are otherwise not very useful compared to Southern women.

Maybe many years from now that child will take her elderly mother by the hand and lead her out on the dance floor to repeat some of those steps I witnessed.

If she does, one thing is for sure and certain.

Everything will still be okay in our homeland.

Down South.

LOOKING SOUTHWARD |

There are people in the world who have never set foot in the Blessed South. Hard to believe, I know, but, sadly, it's true.

I have a dear friend in Colorado who has never been below the Mason-Dixon line.

She often asks me about life in the South. What are the folks like Down South? How's the weather? The food?

She grew up Out West where the mountains are covered with rocks and snowcaps instead of trees. Where the rivers run wild and white rather than muddy and meandering. Where more of the skiing is done on champagne powder than behind a boat on the lake.

Once she asked "What does the South look like?"

It's a great question with thousands of answers.

Here goes.

The South looks like a few million Georgia pines reaching at least a half a mile into a perfect crystal blue sky, the tops of the giant trees swaying to and fro to the gentle breezes that can blow during any season.

The South looks like miles and miles of white sand on the South Carolina coast with warm green ocean water garnished with white sea foam perpetually slapping the beaches. Most days you can watch dolphins. Or are they porpoises? I can never remember. What was Flipper? Anyway, you can usually find them playing in the surf.

Another nearly miraculous view of the South is the seemingly endless pastureland covered with grass that really does look blue, at least from a distance. Kentucky produces the finest horses on the planet and a drive around Lexington is like finding yourself in a picture postcard.

Charleston looks like the South and the South looks like Charleston.

Dozens of picturesque bridges spanning two major rivers and several creeks, thus it's sometimes referred to as The City of Bridges. Drive over the tallest of those bridges and you get a long look at the many spires of the historic old churches that adorn Charleston. That accounts for the official nickname, The Holy City.

Every Southerner should get to experience a magical sunset over Mallory Square in Key West. There's nothing like it anywhere else in the world. And once the sun is down, the party starts. Every night.

That's what the South looks like in Florida.

The South looks like Bourbon Street. Don't take the kids. It's for grown folks. But you find music and food unique to Dixie.

The South looks like eating a muffuletta or beignets while listening to real New Orleans jazz played by ancient looking men while you sit in a cramped and dingy room on a side street and feel blessed to have gotten a table.

The South looks like a massive granite formation known to Southerners as Stone Mountain where a carving of two generals and one confederate president makes the one of four presidents on Rushmore look small by comparison. The South most definitely looks like the panoramic view from the top of that big rock where you can see fifty or more miles in each direction on a clear day.

The Southland looks like a long leisurely drive along the high roads of the Blue Ridge Parkway through the lush mountains and green valleys. Or through the fertile country of the Shenandoah Valley where the farms look pretty much like they did a hundred years ago.

The Mighty Mississippi River, also known as The Big Muddy, taking it's own sweet time, never in much of a hurry, but finally reaching the Gulf of Mexico. That looks like the South.

Or the huge cargo ships chugging out of, or easing into the Port of Galveston down Texas way, or the Port of Savannah, loaded down with freight, coming from or headed to Lord knows where.

That looks like the South to me.

The South also looks like clay so red that if you get it on your white pants it's ain't coming out.

Catfish so ugly only a mother could love it but served up with grits and hushpuppies it becomes a thing of beauty.

Churches full on Sunday mornings, bellies way full after Sunday dinners.

These are just a few glimpses of the South. Mostly, to me, after so many years living away, the South looks like something else.

It looks like home.

I'm certain that my curious Western friend will have more questions about our homeland, yours and mine.

What does the South sound like? Smell like? Taste like?

Great questions.

For another day

Southern Predestination Defined |

There are certain things about living in the Blessed South that are simply inevitable.

Unavoidable.

Inescapable.

Things that may, or may not occur in other parts of the country but, if you reside around here they are bound to happen to you sooner or later.

Like hitting a deer on the highway. If you haven't already, it's just a matter of time. At the very least you've probably run through the nasty mess of a deer somebody else hit. Or, you hit the buzzard dining on the deer that somebody else hit.

Unless you never take your vehicle off the blacktop, one day you'll get stuck in a mud hole or sand bed. It doesn't matter how powerful your four wheel drive is, when you bury it above the axle you'll be on the cell calling the last old boy you pulled out of the ditch to come a-runnin'.

Around these parts you'll find yourself annually praying for rain because of a drought.

A few weeks later the farmers among us will be praying for it to quit raining so they can tend their crops.

It's just a part of life here.

One day you'll buy a boat.

After all, you live within a pebble toss of hundreds of navigable bodies of water that really need navigating. By you. You may sell your boat for half what you paid for it after one or two summers, but you will buy one if you live here a while.

You'll also buy a pickup.

You don't need one. You never haul anything. You never tow anything. Every tool you own would fit in the pocket (known to Yankees as the glove compartment) of your sedan, but one day you'll buy a big, gas guzzling, shiny new American built truck.

Just cause.

And sooner or later you'll stick your truck in a mud hole or sand bed.

And you'll probably hit a deer or two.

Spend much time around here and one day you'll be moseying along minding your own business when your foot suddenly sinks into the ground.

A fire ant bed.

Well, "bed" doesn't really describe it. It's more like a den. A den of iniquity. Evil little demons they are, and sooner or later they'll adorn your foot with painful, itchy little blisters.

It happens to us all.

You'll remember at one minute after 10PM that you need something from the store and then realize that everything is closed. The streets and sidewalks have been rolled up. The businesses locked and shuttered. You're going to have to do without whatever that something is.

This ain't New York City, boys and girls.

Around the end of July you'll start to get all excited about your favorite college football team and their prospects for winning a national championship. Then, around the end of September, when your team has lost two out of five, you're forced into a realistic reassessment.

Here in the Southern countryside you'll step outside one morning and find you're the proud new owner of one, or two, or three stray dogs that some lowlife has dumped out on your road. Several sets of sad eyes looking to you to be their savior.

It's just a part of your Dixie destiny.

Yes, some things just seem to be preordained and there's

nothing you can do to prevent them. But don't fret too mightily, because most clouds do indeed have a sterling lining.

For instance, your team will almost always end the season on a high note, beating some team wearing orange or yellow uniforms.

Yellow uniforms? Really?

The rain might hang around a little too long, but the sound of thunder rolling across the sky starting somewhere around Chattanooga and ending over Charleston makes it okay.

That boat you bought, before you realize you can't afford it, takes you to places impossible to see from the highways. Rivers. Lakes. Intercoastal waterways. All waiting for you to explore.

Fire ants. Okay, there's no upside to fire ants. None whatsoever, and, if they suddenly disappeared from the ecosystem tomorrow, I'd shout Hallelujah for a month of Sundays.

But one dewy morning when you drive by, the deer that survive the road wars will be standing in the edge of a foggy pine thicket, watching you pass, looking for all the world like a Windberg painting. Just for a few seconds. Just for you.

While you're waiting for somebody to come pull you out of that mud hole, you and your passenger buddies might enjoy an impromptu tailgate party.

That pickup truck, well, you still don't need it. But you have it. And sometimes, just having something you worked for is a gracious plenty.

And Down South, it's inevitable.

THE WAY AROUND HERE |

If you're from around Dixie there are certain things that are just understood to be a part of our civilization. Somewhere along the line growing up Southern, though it's doubtful that you could pinpoint exactly when it happened, certain bits of knowledge just became a part of your being. And certain occurrences became the norm.

For instance, if you grew up pretty much anywhere south of the Mason-Dixon line you call people older than you are ma'am or sir. It's a show of respect, just as you refer to older cousins as Aunt or Uncle, never by their first name only.

You've always done it, you always will.

Let's face it, to have been blessed with Southern citizenship, you were born to be unique.

Different.

A little bit red no matter what your race.

A little bit country no matter how big the city you grew up in.

A whole lot proud, and thankful, that you weren't born a Yankee.

Admit it. You have a relative named Bubba. Or you know somebody named Bubba. Maybe your name is Bubba.

Down South it's not just a nickname.

" Mr. and Mrs. Bubba Jones announce the birth of their son, Bubba Jones, Jr."

I know at least a half dozen Bubbas. So do you.

Our priorities run a little different around here too.

Many of us have a much greater interest in music than we do in history and culture.

For example you might not know who George Bernard Shaw is, but you know who George Strait is. You might not be able to identify which president Zachary Taylor was, but you know without a doubt who Zach Brown is. You may not even know what part Dolly Madison played in American history, no, she didn't event the snack cake, but you know durn good and well who Dolly Parton is.

Nothing wrong with that. George, Zach and Dolly will all be part of Southern American history one day.

If you're a true Southerner you know how to shag.

Okay, get your minds out of the gutter boys and girls.

I'm not referring to the course term invented by some movie director for the silly Austin Powers movies of the nineties.

And I don't mean those hideous layered haircuts that we all thought were so cool back in the day.

I'm talking about the official state dance of the Carolinas, North and South. You can see the Carolina Shag being done, and done well, on the boardwalks and dance floors all along the sandy white coastline from Surf City down through Myrtle Beach and all the way to Beaufort.

Our Carolinian neighbors even allow shagging outside of their state borders on holiday weekends.

Southerners shag.

You've eaten frog legs. And chitlins. And crawdads. You may have even swallowed a few raw oysters. You might also have had to fight back the urge to regurgitate after any one of those slimy dining adventures like I did with each and every one, but you still did it.

Cause you're Southern.

You pull over to the side of the road when a funeral approaches. You may not know the deceased from Adam's housecat but you show your respect by getting off the road. If somebody goes around you and doesn't pull over, check the license plate. Most likely the car will be from somewhere outside of the Blessed South.

At least once a week, after dark, you have to slow way down when you see bright eyes shining ahead of you. Deer. What is it about the side of the road that deer find so irresistible when they have millions of acres of woods to roam in?

Southerners, at the first chords of the national anthem, automatically remove their hats and place their hands over their hearts. That's simple patriotism.

On the other hand, if you hold dual citizenship and your other beloved homeland is Margaritaville, when you hear Jimmy crooning that anthem, you instinctively feel compelled to remove your shoes and stick your toes in the sand.

You can't help it.

That's how we roll.

For the record, Zachary Taylor was the twelfth president of the United States, the last elected from the South until 114 years later. He reportedly had two cousins, one uncle and one coon hound all named Bubba. The uncle was, of course called Uncle Bubba, sir.

I doubt that old Zachary ever shagged but I suspect that he did eat his share of chitlins.

After all, he was from the South.

Shopping In The Country |

They are often the social crossroads of the communities that they serve.

You can drop in for some quick shopping or a cup of coffee. Or maybe just for some company and conversation.

You'll often find a few folks there who have come just to sip and catch up on the latest news or gossip.

There's plenty of both at the little businesses and it's likely you'll know most of the other customers.

Country stores.

The words bring to mind Mary Jane candies and six ounce bottles, real glass bottles, of Coke. Or wood plank floors and drink cartons turned upright and used as stools. Or Dreamsicles and Hunky ice cream bars.

Country stores have a charm about them that, with all due respect, you won't find at the convenience stores in cities, though some do try.

I once visited a little Mom and Pop store near downtown Philadelphia that was simply named The Country Store. There wasn't a dirt road within fifty miles and I seriously doubt that they sold cane poles.

I can't envision any store in the rural South calling itself The City Store.

When I was growing up on the farm we had a little store right across the road from us. Long gone now, it was known as Scott's Store and later as Shell Bluff Grocery.

Mister Scott's was without doubt the meeting place of our little community. He was a very big man with white hair and a glass eye that was always looking right at me. He told me that he lost his eye while he was looking down the barrel of the rifle he was cleaning. He often warned me never to engage in such foolish activity. Knowing now what I do about old men and tall tales, I don't know if the story was true, but I've never once looked down the barrel of a loaded weapon.

That glass eye spooked me.

On rainy days the farmers would sometimes gather at the store. Some would have the proverbial Moon Pie and RC Cola. Daddy always got peanut brittle. Others would buy a pack of salted peanuts and pour them into one of the above mentioned six ounce bottles of Coke, then would drink and eat at the same time, a Southern thang, no doubt.

The drinks were kept in a huge cooler in cold water, not ice. Water so cold your hand hurt when you reached in for a bottle.

For the older farmers whose few remaining teeth could not handle the brittle or nuts, there were always fresh bananas.

Something for everybody.

My favorite was Stage Plank cookies. I ate dozens of them over the years while listening to the men argue and cuss.

Yes, there was plenty of cussing, in fact the store is where I learned the art of proper cussing.

If they weren't cussing the rain they were cussing the drought.

If they weren't cussing the Democrats they were cussing the Republicans.

If they weren't cussing Yankees they were cussing boll weevils, both of which were considered equally harmful to Southern life.

The cussing reached historic levels when gasoline hit thirtyone cents a gallon.

Wow.

I once asked Daddy why those old men cussed so much. He explained that they weren't really cussing, they were DIScussing, and left it at that.

Back when "going to town" was quite an ordeal, country stores dotted the rural landscape every few miles and were precursors of modern day chains like 7-11 and Golden Pantry. Nowadays, we think nothing of hopping in our vehicles and driving in for whatever we need.

There are fewer country stores today but the ones still around are pretty much the same as they always were, just a bit shinier.

At the one in my community you can choose your bait. Red wigglers, pinks, or crickets. You'll also find a few fishing lures.

The coffee is strong but most of the time it's fresh. You won't find a cappuccino or espresso machine.

There's still good talk and good company. The lady proprietor will tell me in a heartbeat if she didn't particularly like what I wrote some week. Other weeks she liked it fine. That's alright with me.

There's still occasional cussing but not in front of the ladies and not at the rain.

These days we never cuss the rain.

You can still get a Moon Pie or Stage Plank, but these days I also get a lecture along with my purchase from the proprietor's granddaughter telling me how bad such sugar laden fare is for me.

That's okay too.

At least she doesn't have a scary glass eye.

How It's Done Around Here |

The young man sitting across the desk from me, his desk, not mine, was listening politely. Intently. He was hearing me and understanding exactly what it was I was proposing. But every now and then I caught a flicker of a look that told me something else. I couldn't quite place it until the third or fourth time I saw it. Then I knew it wasn't my imagination.

No, the look was real and I'd seen it before.

He was trying to decide if I was serious.

Or if I was addlebrained.

Truth is, I probably am, but he didn't know me well enough to be privy to that information.

Of course, ours is a small town, so maybe he'd heard the rumors.

Anyway, he allowed me to finish my spiel.

All I wanted was to borrow a quarter of a million dollars from his bank to build my dream house.

I should mention here that "my" dream house was one that I found in a log home catalog, designed by some nameless architect, being sold by an out-of-state corporation to eventually be built by craftsmen from other parts of the country, possibly even Yankees.

A kit house.

Once I finished my presentation the young banker leaned back in his chair and was silent for all of five seconds. Then he leaned forward.

" Well, you certainly qualify for that much. Your credit rating is very good. I'm sure we can work out all the details."

I only allowed myself to relax halfway. I've been reading people's body language long enough to know that there was a very big and important "but" that was about to follow the good news.

It came, but it wasn't anything I expected.

He continued, " But, why would you want to?"

" Say what?" I thought to myself. " Wasn't he paying attention to my golden tongue?"

" Why? I want to build the house I just described and that's how much it's going to cost."

Now it was his turn to talk.

In a nutshell he explained, based on what I had told him I wanted, that I could hire a local builder, design my own house, bigger and nicer than the one I'd shown him, for a little more than half of what I'd proposed.

See, that's what I like about being back around these parts.

That would not have happened in the big city banks I've dealt with in the past. They'd have loaned me the money and basically abandoned me until a payment was five minutes late getting to them.

He could have loaned and left too. But he didn't.

I like that.

And I liked his idea so I drove to my favorite lunch spot and started to draw up a floor plan.

The place has been there as long as I've been alive and has changed very little. My earliest memory of eating anywhere other than Mama's table was there. I gazed out at the same grassy shore and the same weedy lake that I've known forever. It was a comfortable feeling.

I like that too.

I did come up with my own floor plan as I sat there eating my hamburger steak with gravy and fries enjoying every juicy, small town, rural South, cholesterol laden morsel of it.

Health risk notwithstanding, something about the day just felt right.

That happens a lot lately.

I go into a store and invariably run into an old buddy or gal pal. We stand there for half an hour gossiping and telling each other how great we look.

I drive downtown and travel through a tree tunnel that has shaded part of main street since before my granddaddies were born. I've passed under it a jillion times.

I go to a local game. Half the players are the kids of old schoolmates which gives me the perfect right to cuss out the referees with the rest of the crowd.

And now I'm living in that real dream house. It stands near the spot where I played on the old sawdust pile as a kid, on land that's been in my family for hundreds of years. The homestead has enough bedrooms so that when my kids invade from every other time zone in America there'll be plenty of room.

Crickets and cicadas will sing me to sleep most summer nights.

Soon, there will be a tire swing hanging from a sturdy limb somewhere.

Another tree will bear the initials of my little lineage carved into the bark down through the decades.

It all seems to be coming together now. Slowly. Gradually. Life I mean, this stanza of it back home where it began.

Addlebrained or not, I like that. A lot.

Say It Southern |

"He don't know the difference between a hay fork and a manure fork".

The old cattleman was voicing his exasperation about his farm hand who also happened to be his son.

I chuckled because I'd never heard that particular lament before but there was no misunderstanding the meaning.

The boy was ignorant. I never found out whether he really confused the two barnyard implements but the point was made.

Southerners have all sorts of colorful expressions to describe, without subtlety, how we truly feel about certain individuals. Often the sayings are followed by the obligatory " Bless his/her heart" refrain.

"That boy is dumber than a box of rocks", is one that I've heard many times, fortunately never directed toward myself. It's pretty self explanatory. What could be dumber than a crate full of chunks of inanimate geologic material?

A nice variation of the same theme is " You two are dumber than a bag of hammers". I first heard that one in a movie about the South. It's become a popular one since. Hammers only serve one purpose. To hit things. I suppose if you are less intelligent than a hammer you serve NO purpose.

Point taken.

Every Southerner has a favorite when referring to the

brightness challenged among us. I once told Daddy that I was thinking of going into partnership with a friend who owned a chicken farm in Alabama. Keep in mind he'd been trying to get some farming out of me for years.

"Well son, that's a job that requires a strong back and a weak mind", he said.

I honestly don't know if he was dissing chicken farmers or allowing that he thought I was qualified.

While folks who appear to be feebleminded do bring forth many fine Southernisms such as " He couldn't find his butt with both hands", the truly insane ones inspire even more.

"That woman is crazy as a sprayed roach", was one that I heard when I lived in South Georgia. It didn't make a lot of sense the first time I heard it but it does now. Get the Raid after one of the ugly little crawlers and take note of the resemblance to some of your eccentric relatives. I've witnessed it. So have you. Scary.

"Crazy as a bedbug" is another.

And "Crazy as a guinea wasp" or it's variation " As (messed) up as a guinea wasp".

I thought that one was just made up until I looked up guinea wasps and found out that they really do exist, though I have no idea as to the breed's level of lunacy.

Seems as though insect life is the common denominator for describing nutcases throughout the Blessed South.

A person's finances, or lack thereof, can illicit some pointed phrases with that unique Southern slant.

"I'm more broke than all ten commandments", I once heard a cousin say when he was asked by his buddies to purchase a round.

That's pretty broke.

"She's so poor she can't even pay attention". Overheard at church.

No doubt, Down South, if a condition fits at least one human being, we will find a down home way to describe it.

You want to tell somebody about an acquaintance who puts on airs and pretends to be something he's not? It's simple.

"Big Stetson, no cattle".

You want to emphasize the seriousness of somebody's level of intoxication?

"He was drunker than Hogan's goat".

I have no idea who Hogan was or why his goat was hammerfaced, but the indication is crystal clear.

You don't recognize somebody?

"I don't know her from Adam's housecat".

Adam lived in a garden till his well documented eviction. Far as I know he didn't have a house and presumably no housecat either. That explains the unfamiliarity.

You notice a fellow standing on the corner displaying a huge toothy smile for no obvious reason.

"He's grinning like a jackass eating briers." This guy could also very possibly be " A dime short of a dollar".

Approach with caution.

You have a friend who is, shall we say, lacking in physical appearance.

" Uglier than a mud fence".

That's another one I didn't understand till the first time I saw a mud fence.

Yep, pretty homely.

The list of colloquialisms is endless. Makes a boy proud to be from Dixie.

By the way, the difference between a hay fork and a manure fork is pretty easy to distinguish.

One smells worse than the other.

If you didn't already know that...bless your heart.

SOUTHERN RESISTANCE |

" Hey yall, watch this!"

Jeff Foxworthy attributes that exclamation to many rednecks shouting their last words.

He got it right.

Lots of country Southern males who proudly claim redneck status find it difficult to resist any opportunity to showcase a little backwoods bravado.

It might be by finding an eight foot alligator and deciding to tease it for a while with a hoe handle until it turns that object into toothpicks. It wasn't a particularly intelligent thing to do but it was pretty fascinating to witness.

It could be attempting to swing across a gully on a vine to celebrate a 50th birthday.

Or jumping over a campfire just because somebody said you couldn't. I only missed by a foot, and only scorched one boot.

Southern maleness knows no age, race or religion.

Or intelligence level.

Incidentally, I mentioned country Southern males because it seems that all boys and men around these parts either claim to be from the country or have learned to act country. Can't blame them. Who in his right mind would profess to be a city boy?

Here's a list of items that Southern country boys find very tough to resist.

Mama's cooking. Every son of the South believes that his mama is the world's greatest cook. Contrary to Hollywood's portrayal of our homeland, most of us don't eat possum grits or bologna cake. But everybody's mama prepares the best fried chicken or country ham known to man. Her desserts are legendary too. Pecan pies or coconut cakes that make you cry. Who could resist?

Dirt roads. I love to drive the river roads on my side of the county, some of which are still unpaved. I hope they stay that way. Southern country boys love dirt roads. Drive down any one of them and you'll see evidence of circles being spun by pick up trucks or four wheel drive vehicles. I can't swear that all of the steel belted radial artwork was left by country boys but it's a good bet that it wasn't aliens or Yankees.

Rebel Yells. Nowadays also known as redneck yells. What country boy hasn't at some time in his life bellowed out a wahoo or shrieked to the top of his lungs for no other reason but to celebrate being a human being free on the Earth. I have, plenty of times.

Shooting road signs. I know. It's destructive. It's probably at least a misdemeanor in most counties and it's not the safest sport in the world. But it's hard to resist. Don't believe me? Pay attention the next time you take a ride through the countryside and see how many signs display somebody's marksmanship.

Mud holes. Drive through any high school parking lot after a rainy weekend and see how many pickups are covered with red clay or yellow mud. They didn't get that way parked on a paved driveway. The more mud covering the multi thousand dollar paint job the cooler the truck. People have spent entire Saturdays competing in events to see whose vehicle could make it across a bog. A glorified mud hole.

Camouflage clothes. Even Southern country boys who have never hunted, never cut a wild hair or feather (granted there can't be too many such beings Down South) seem compelled to dress in camo at least once a week. And deer season? A stranger to the area would swear that he had stumbled into the middle of somebody's private war where every male from 9 to 90 is clad in the green, brown and black patterned attire. Everybody looks good in camo.

Burning rubber. I have a couple of nephews who contribute

more to Goodyear annually than Dale Earnhardt, Jr. Enough said.

Noise. Southern country boys like it loud. I can always tell when one of those nephews gets home. He lives near me and I can hear him coming from a half mile away. Sometimes it's rap, sometimes country. Sometimes it's unidentifiable to anybody over 18. Good ole boys, makin' noise. Loud music. Loud mufflers. And of course there are loud mouths the number of which is incalculable. Boys down South like to be heard.

Telling whoppers, AKA tall tales, AKA lies. This is an art form in Dixie that every Southern boy possesses. Sometimes it's hard to distinguish a tall tale, for instance a story about killing an attacking bobcat with a boat paddle, from an outright lie, like denying you voted for Bill Clinton. Or George Bush. I, myself, try to avoid any kind of untruths, preferring to stick to just the facts in my tale telling.

Southern country girls. This one requires no explanation.

Resistance is futile.

V

THE LORD,
THE CHURCH AND
PRAYING UP A STORM

*"Save me, oh God, from people
who have no sense of humor."*

~ Ludlow Porch ~

The Praying Contest |

When I was thirteen years old, without consulting me first, my appendix decided to bust wide open. I never found out what causes that to happen, and, from what I understand, medical science still doesn't know.

I just knew it hurt.

I'd been having pains in my side for weeks but had ignored them until it got so bad that I wasn't able to participate in the annual Turkey Bowl football game at Grandma's house on Thanksgiving Day. That's when Mama decided that I needed to see the doctor.

We drove to town to see Doc Lamar. After he had done a lot of prodding around he announced that I had a ruptured appendix. It appeared to have been ruptured for two weeks and would require immediate surgery. He told us that had we waited one more day I might have succumbed.

When I learned what succumbed meant I nearly died. I knew Jesus by that age and had been baptized in the muddy waters of Brier Creek under Thompson's Bridge, but I was nowhere near ready to go to Heaven!

I was a kid! I wanted to live forever!

They immediately sent me to the hospital where we were met by Doc Walter, the surgeon. During his examination he told me that the fat pocket around my middle probably kept the poison from the rupture from spreading and killing me. I really wanted them all to stop talking about death! But, it was the only time in my life I've been thankful for a big belly.

Later, I was laying alone in the surgery prep ward when a huge male nurse walked in holding a straight razor. "I'm here for your shave son" was all he said. This was the 60's and all I knew about straight razors was that only hoodlums and bikers carried them. If the two Docs hadn't already scared me this fellow had me terrified. But, he did shave me from mid chest to my knees without missing a hair, leaving everything else where it belonged.

The surgery was done that same day and it was successful and removed all of the offending organ but I had to stay in the hospital for nearly two weeks until the toxins cleared out.

One afternoon a nurse came in and asked me if I had been to the bathroom that day. I told her that I hadn't been since the surgery.

That fact seemed to concern her greatly so she left but returned in a few minutes. She brought back a pill that she said was necessary based on the information I had provided her. It wasn't the kind of pill you swallow. I won't say how she administered it except to say that it was quite uncomfortable. Then she slid a big silver bedpan under me and left the room. I found out later why she left.

Shortly after that the preacher from my church, Pastor Jimmy, arrived accompanied by the Methodist minister, Reverend Henry. They were followed by the Catholic priest, Father John. Mama didn't allow us to call him Father since we were Baptists, but I did anyway cause I thought he was cool. With Father John was the hospital chaplain whose name I never knew.

They gathered around my bed and began to chat with each other which was fine with me since I was about to doze off. Then Pastor Jimmy suggested that they pray over me. He wanted the Lord to know how thankful they all were that I had been snatched away from almost certain death.

There was that word again!

Well, they started to pray and to call on the Powers That Be to heal my young body and to do so quickly.

They all prayed at once and it appeared to me that they were actually trying to outpray each other! It was a sight to behold and something to hear! A praying contest beseeching God on my behalf!

Till it happened. That pill that the nurse gave me kicked in and worked like a charm. The preachers didn't notice at first but then Pastor Jimmy paused his imploring to catch his breath and at the same time caught a whiff of what gets stored up inside a sick boy who hasn't been to the outhouse lately.

When they all became aware of what had happened they all hollered "Amen" in unison and stampeded for the door .

I suddenly realized, that with one involuntary bodily function, I had done what millions of churchgoers have wished they could accomplish on many longwinded Sunday mornings.

I laughed so hard I would've busted my appendix except I didn't have one to spare.

COUNTRY PREACHING |

Country preachers are a different breed with different circumstances and problems than their city counterparts.

In an earlier time it was customary for country preachers to live in houses on the church property, once known as pastoriums. Oddly, that word no longer appears in either Webster's or Oxford dictionaries. Should be somewhere between pastille and pasturage. Don't bother looking. It's not there.

Anyway, while country churches all over the South offered free housing to the pastors, there was a downside.

If you occupied the pastorium you were likely to live across the road from a graveyard.

While such "residents" close by would make for quiet neighbors, I personally wouldn't be comfortable living so close. When I get tired of my living and breathing kin or friends I can politely ask them to immediately vacate the premises. Not so if you live just over the pavement from acres full of deceased ones.

They ain't going anywhere.

Sharing your grounds with the saints gone before is not for the faint of heart.

Country preachers have to be tough since their "flock" can sometimes be a bit rough around the edges.

I often attended services at a small country congregation in the Rockies where the pastor was a close friend. The community had only a few hundred residents, many of whom worked in the nearby mines. Miners are hard folks and my friend's congregants kept him plenty busy.

One Sunday as the invitation was being offered, I heard the floorboards of the old building creaking behind me as if they were about to shatter under whatever load they were bearing. I glanced back and saw a huge man slowly making his way down the aisle. He was at least six feet six inches tall and weighed over three hundred pounds. He was a miner I'd met who had recently started coming to church. He was a loud, coarse, hard drinking and harder living man.

When he passed by I saw him wiping tears from his eyes with hands the size of Boston butts.

Salvation.

He wanted to be baptized right away even though it was wintertime in Colorado and the baptistery was unheated. They made their way into the pool with the newly saved miner towering over the preacher who was half his size. My friend took the confession and with all his strength laid the miner back and pushed him under the near icy water.

When he came up out of the water the man was sputtering and cussing like only a coal miner can with one fist balled up like he might punch my friend for trying to freeze or drown him.

Without a second's hesitation my friend shoved the man back under and held him down a few seconds longer. He looked out into the congregation and said "The first one obviously didn't take!"

The second time the fellow came out of the water he was a bit more sheepish. I hope that he has had a peaceful earthly walk cause his spiritual beginning was anything but.

Years ago we had a pastor who was related to several members of the church, a real fire and brimstone speaker. Every Sunday he would rattle the rafters like thunder. One day during a particularly animated oration he slammed his fist down on the wooden podium so hard that he broke his watchband, and probably his wrist, and woke up a couple of dozing deacons, one of whom stood up and opened his hymn book a bit prematurely. I'm sure it hurt but the preacher just flipped the watch aside and preached on.

Another time a young minister was baptizing a very elderly

gentleman in Briar Creek when a strong current ripped the man from his grip. He practically had to dive in to retrieve the new saint but he got the job done with no loss of life.

I doubt that's ever happened at a mega church in a big city.

I know another minister who preaches full time and also runs a full time business. He once fought off two attackers who intended to rob him.

One gun. One knife. One tough preacher man.

He was stabbed and seriously injured but was back in the pulpit long before his wounds healed.

He gave all the credit to the Lord. I agree. I credit Him with giving the pastor the strength to battle back and to save his own life.

Tough.

Meaning no disrespect to city churches but it's hard to beat a good country preacher.

I know of two robbers and a coal miner who will attest.

Dinner On The Grounds |

The event has changed a bit over the years.

It was once held under the old oak trees on the east side of the building. These days it takes place close to the same spot, but now it's an inside affair.

Before, folks were drafted to be the designated gnat and fly fanners. They stood along the edges of the tables protecting the innumerable dishes of food from the flying pests until grace was asked and the partaking began.

Nowadays the food doesn't require much fanning since the gathering is inside the climate controlled, multi-use facility.

Years ago the only time the events were held indoors was when it rained. Then we'd have to cram all the food, folks and folding tables inside the only additional space, other than the sanctuary, an old Army barracks converted to a classroom facility.

The ways and the means of the event might have evolved with the times, but the event itself hasn't changed and neither has the name.

Dinner On The Grounds.

When I heard those words as a kid I would start looking forward to it weeks in advance. I always knew that there would be plenty of good food and friends, and, though I didn't really know what the word meant back then, good fellowship.

Back when the dinners were still held outside there was a lag time between when the preacher finally said amen and when the eating began. The kids would play football, or tag, or catch while the adults prepared the feast.

One year somebody produced a Frisbee and we began tossing it around. Mama made a point of telling us not to throw "that thing" near the food. I wasn't good with a Frisbee but was giving it my best effort when I let one fly. It went out of control and headed toward the tables where at least a hundred people were crowded around. As though it had radar, it picked Mama out of the crowd and bounced right off the top of her home perm. I tried to run and hide but I was frozen. Everybody laughed.

Except Mama.

Good Baptists, and I suspect folks from all denominations, will use any excuse to have a good old potluck dinner. Fifth Sunday. Homecoming. Revival. People like to gather.

I hadn't been to one at my home church in a while and I was really looking forward to the most recent one. I wasn't disappointed.

The service before the dinner was a music special by a group of very talented voices singing old time gospel numbers. That was followed by over a half dozen baptisms, lots of clapping and rejoicing.

There's no better place on Earth to worship than a little country church, and no finer get together than a dinner on the grounds.

I found Aunt Clara's famous potato salad on one of the tables. She's been gone for several years but the tradition endures through her children. It was as good as always.

There were dozens of salads, vegetable dishes, casseroles, ten different varieties of fried chicken, sliced ham, cocktail weenies, even pigs in a blanket.

The dessert table was loaded down with all sorts of cakes, peach cobblers, pies. A billion mouthwatering calories.

There would be no need for a miracle involving five loaves and two fishes on this day.

I loaded down my plate and sat with a family I have known my whole life. Many of the folks there were ones I have known forever.

Having lived away for many years has not lessened how I feel about them, and, it seems to be okay with most of them that I've "come home".

While I chatted with my friends up walked three ladies, a woman and her two daughters. Though I hadn't seen any of them for years, time didn't seem to matter. She and her late husband were friends with Mama and Daddy. The daughters babysat me when the grownups went out together. Back then I thought of them as the coolest, prettiest girls I'd ever seen. I have to admit that I was a mite disconcerted by the fact that both of them looked considerably younger than me, but it was a fine little mini reunion.

That's how it has always been and how it will always be at a dinner on the grounds. We no longer have to dodge bugs and raindrops, but not much else has changed. Wonderful friends. Great conversation. Overeating. Fellowship.

And not a gnat to be seen.

Or a Frisbee.

I Pray He Laughs |

I'm pretty sure that I'm going to Heaven.

In fact, I'm as certain as I think it's possible to be.

But, if for some reason my final destination is the least bit in doubt, I can pinpoint one of the reasons. I understand that Heavenly residence does not require a sinless life and that no single event can cause you to be fire and brimstone bound rather than eastern skyward when you die.

But some things, on the face of them, simply seem a little worse than others.

I have one of those moments in my past. A dark moment that makes me hope God truly does have a sense of humor.

More about that in a bit.

Speaking of praying, if you grew up in a country church in the Blessed South you have, no doubt, experienced sitting through seemingly endless, sermonic prayers that were supposed to end the church service but actually seemed to extend it by half.

Years ago we had a gentleman in our little congregation whose name I dreaded hearing called to close the service because, if it was Sunday morning I would be starving before we finally made it to dinner and if it was Sunday night we were going to miss the first part of Bonanza.

He was a godly man, no doubt, but a long winded one. He literally preached his own little sermonette between " Dear Lord" and " Amen ". He was not shy about correcting the pastor while talking to the Lord if he'd taken exception to anything that had been preached that day. But the strangest part was when he would quote scripture during his entreaties.

"Almighty Father, it says in Isaiah 5:11..."

I'd think, " I'm sure God knows what it says since He wrote it!"

That sweet old saint was responsible for dozens of overcooked Sunday dinners.

Prayers are serious, obviously, but, because they're offered by man and not by angels, they don't always go as intended.

Once, before a family meal, my brother Willie was called on to pray. My grandmother was quite elderly by that time and she had been snacking a bit before the meal had actually commenced. As Willie was asking God's blessings on the bounty before us, my grandmother let out a loud belch.

Willie didn't miss a beat.

"...and we also thank you for the part that Grandma already ate. Amen."

As long as there are flawed humans doing the praying, there's always the possibility that things might go a bit askew.

Which brings me back to the grievous event from my past.

When I was in college I ran around with a group of friends, most of who shared my beliefs. We often enjoyed impromptu Bible studies and devotionals together.

One day we were at Watson's Mill Bridge State Park, a beautiful setting a few miles from campus. Somebody suggested a prayer time. We found a nice, grassy area by the creek and settled down.

Back then I would not always close my eyes to pray, preferring to look out on His creation. When it came to my turn I began with thankfulness for our magnificent surroundings. As I prayed I opened my eyes to gaze at the flowing water and when I did I sensed movement below me so I glanced down.

That's when things went terribly wrong.

There, directly between my feet, lay my least favorite of His creations.

A water moccasin staring at me with his wicked little eyes.

Before I could stop it my twenty year old, farmboy/college

student mouth let loose with a barnyard bad word that Mama would have smacked me for saying anywhere, let alone in the middle of a prayer session.

I cussed much louder than I'd been praying.

I couldn't help it.

Every last one of my companions looked at me, stunned, but then looked down and saw the subject of my nasty epitaph. None of them cussed, but the whole bunch fled the scene, all howling and laughing like crazy folks.

"Did you just cuss in a prayer?" asked one of my girl buddies, giggling nearly uncontrollably.

"I don't think it's technically possible to cuss and pray at the same time," I postulated while beating my own hasty retreat.

To this day I'm convinced that the snake was the serpent of Scripture come to test me.

I failed.

But I'm pretty sure that the nanosecond that the cuss word flew from my immediately remorseful lips, the praying ended.

We later finished our prayers from the top of a picnic table. My friends had a good laugh at my expense.

Hopefully, God did too.

SING IT OUT |

"Night with ebon pinion,
Brooded o'er the vale,
All around was silent,
Save the night winds wail..."

After a long absence I am once again singing in the choir at the little country church where I grew up.

I'm loving it.

Church music has changed over the years with a more modern sound being the favored kind of congregational singing.

Praise and worship music is now a multi million dollar industry.

I like the new upbeat songs.

But I also like the old standards and hymns that we once sang in my early years in the choir.

I'm not alone.

"Southern Gospel Music" appears to be as strong as ever.

Many of the old songs, like the one referenced above, sometimes had us singing words and phrases with no clue as to the meaning, but the poetry was so haunting that nobody cared.

What exactly does "ebon pinion" mean anyway?

I know at least two motorheads in the choir who would immediately tell you that a pinion is a part of a gear drive train. Ebon, obviously a derivative of ebony, means black.

A black drive train?

Don't think so.

Over the years I have often picked up old hymnals just to read some of the words and while doing so recently, I was reminded of times when the words of a song were either mispronounced, misunderstood or misused.

Sometimes all of the above.

"Bringing in the sheaves, bringing in the sheaves, we shall come rejoicing, bringing in the sheaves."

Nearly every child I ever knew, including all three of my own, at one time or another belted out:

"Bringing in the sheep, bringing in the sheep..."

They knew what the wooly livestock creatures were. They'd seen them at the stock shows, but had never laid eyes on one sheaf, let alone sheaves.

As a kid I remember singing ... " there my ruptured soul shall find, rest beyond the river."

I knew what ruptured meant. It's what could happen to your boy parts if you do an incorrect cannonball off the high dive, but I had no idea what "raptured" meant.

After my unfortunate rendition Mama explained the difference in no uncertain terms.

One year my older brother and I were working in the fields on separate tractors. It was hot and dusty and we were sweltering. This was long before the advent of enclosed, air conditioned cabs. We had been hoping, just like every day, that it would rain and get us out of the sun for a while.

Sure enough, early that afternoon, it began to cloud up. Down came a few drops, then a steady drizzle. I parked my tractor at the end of a row under a tree and shut it down.

I spotted Urb headed my way and could hear him singing over the noise of the old Ford 9000.

"Showers of blessings, showers of blessings we need. Mercy drops round us are falling, but for the showers we plead."

I suspect that's not how the author of that wonderful old number intended it to be utilized, but, there were never two farm boys more thankful for a mercifully cooling downpour.

When my oldest daughter had been reading for a couple of

years she was so proud when she could hold her own songbook in church with no assistance from her mother or me. She could read the words and, even at a young age, had a melodious voice.

One Sunday the song leader began one of the old songs. My daughter was keeping up and keeping tempo.

"There is a fountain filled with blood, drawn from Emmanuel's veins. And sinners plunged beneath that flood, lose all their guilty stains".

There was a slight pause during which the literal ramifications of the words she had just uttered sunk into her young brain.

"Gross!" She was seven. She was loud.

I tried not to but I cracked up. So did everybody within ten pews.

I'm thinking even He got a chuckle out of that.

Later we had a good discussion about baptism and being " washed in the blood" and how many words in church songs and hymns are not always exactly as they appear. We also talked about how some lyrics are "old timey" but still have meanings today.

Like "night, with ebon pinion."

Pinion, in it's use in that song, means a wing. Ebon. A black wing, perhaps a raven's. It signifies a great dark bird casting it's shadow over the gloom that was Gethesemane.

Somber, but beautiful.

I love the old songs. They never grow old.

For instance,

"Amazing grace how sweet the sound, that saved a wreck like me."

Or maybe it's wretch.

Either way works.

Laughing With The Lord |

Going to church, especially in the small country congregations of the Blessed South, was always a very severe exercise.

Solemn and somber.

No room for humor or delight.

After all, church was where you came to be spiritually whupped, twice on Sunday, once midweek, not to be entertained or amused.

Those old time preachers did not believe they were called to coddle. They were ordained to shout out the Word and pound the pulpit, not tell funny stories or spew lighthearted banter.

On any given Sabbath day, at any gathering of any denomination throughout Dixie the rafters would shake, the stained glass would rattle and the listeners would tremble while the good reverends mopped pails of sweat from their brows and preached fire and brimstone.

Worship was serious business.

It's still serious, but somewhere along the way we learned to smile, even laugh, to be joyous in our services.

As far as I know, nobody ever went to hell for telling a funny story in the Lord's house.

But even back in the days of the terrifying men stomping around, bellowing the gospel from the pulpits, funny things happened.

It couldn't be helped. Churches are full of human beings, silly creatures by nature.

Daddy often told a story on his youngest brother who, in his later years, became a minister himself.

One Sunday, my uncle, who was around ten years old, was giving a short lesson to the congregants before the preaching began. He had practiced his little talk and was determined to say the vocal passages by memory rather than read them. He had chosen the story of mighty Samson who fought and defeated the Philistines armed only with the jawbone of an ass, most likely using the King James version to quote the words from the Book of Judges.

When he reached the pivotal verse he got a little confused.

"And Samson took the jawbone of a donkey and whipped the Philistine's asses," he blurted.

My uncle's brothers, Daddy included, were, I'm certain, much like mine, and they never let him forget it as evidenced by the fact that the story is still being told some sixty-five years later.

When I was quite young I was also given an opportunity to speak to the very same church for a few minutes before the sermon began. Like my uncle all those years before I was very prepared. I've long since forgotten the topic or the verses that I selected.

Emotional trauma will do that.

I dressed in my best Sunday clothes. Starched black pants. Starched white shirt. Polished genuine fake leather shoes. A very cool paisley clip on tie.

I was ready!

I even got to sit in one of the cane bottomed chairs right next to the pulpit, facing the audience awaiting my turn to speak, just me and the scary, sweaty preacher.

When my time arrived I proudly walked to the predetermined speaking spot. I stood straight and tall and took a deep breath.

Before I could say a word my big brother and a few cousins began howling. They, for the first time in history, had decided to sit on the front row.

Inches from where I stood.

I was suddenly panic stricken. I hadn't even spoken, what could possibly be so funny?

Urb pointed downward and I immediately got a sick feeling in the pit of my stomach.

I didn't want to look but when I did I beheld my zipper all the way down with the long white shirttail sticking out of it for all the world to see, and as far as I was concerned it might as well have been Earth's entire population.

You think I ever lived that one down, even now?

Nope.

I can laugh about it years later but in all the public speaking I've done down through the years, not once have I ever stood on a stage without first triple checking my fly.

Not once.

So, rightly or wrongly, going to church can be fun, and funny.

Like my friend who slipped and fell coming down the steps of the podium holding a tray of those tiny cups filled with communion juice.

He covered the family sitting on the front row with the purple liquid which was funny enough, but I was the only one close enough to him to hear the whispered dirty word that slipped out, and the follow-up prayer asking forgiveness, all in one breath.

That was funny.

I'm convinced that God has a sense of humor.

So laugh. Smile. Rejoice.

Be happy in the House.

Just be sure to zip up first.

VI
Then And Now

*"Either write something worth reading
or do something worth writing."*

~ Benjamin Franklin ~

THE WINDOW SEAT |

I had just taken my seat on the return flight from my Thanksgiving trip when I began to reflect back on the initial flight
That journey to Dallas had begun with promise. After I'd settled into my window seat and dutifully strapped on my seatbelt, I saw a gorgeous woman making her way down the aisle. Most of the seats around me had been filled except for the other two on my row. As the woman, who was about my age, came closer, I began to bargain with God.

"Okay Lord, just this once, let me be lucky. I've flown millions of miles and not one time, EVER, have I had anyone so good looking sit by me. How about today?"

The lady paused, glanced at some seating numbers and continued walking my direction.

"Yes! Just a little closer. Look to your left. You're in 31E".

She stopped next to me. I held my breath.

"Sir. I've misplaced my glasses. Is this row 21?" The Texas accent was unmistakable.

Nobility overruled my first reaction which was to lie.

"No ma'am. Row 21 is ten rows back toward the front"

She flashed the prettiest smile. " Thank you so much", she drawled as she headed back down the aisle.

Dadgum the luck. Ah well. C'est la vie.

"Oh no!"

Next down the aisle came a woman at least 150 years old. Blue hair. Red rouge on one cheek, the other inexplicably unpainted. Lipstick even redder than the rouge. And perfume so overpowering I first whiffed it from four rows away.

"Please Lord, let her pass on by."

No such luck.

31D. Only one seat between us. Eighteen inches between me and suffocation.

Okay, it's a short flight. Not to worry. If I only breathed once every five heartbeats I'd survive the fumes. The plane was full except for the seat next to me. The crew was preparing to close the doors. At least I'd have a little extra room.

Nope.

Through the doors came the one obligatory late passenger.

"Please, no!"

I'm big but this guy made me look like a Calvin Klein model. Four-hundred pounds easy.

I desperately glanced around to see if I'd overlooked any other empty seats. Nope. Just good old 31E.

The gentleman had to walk sideways down the aisle and still violated the sensibilities of every passenger in an end seat.

After what seemed like two eternities he was standing next to my row with a sympathetic smile on his face, even bigger up close.

"There is no way on God's green earth...wait...my Discman!"

I snatched it out of his seat just before it was crushed to dust.

The next second I found myself plastered against the window with no hope of escape for the next two hours and eighteen minutes.

Could this flight get any worse? Oh yea.

My new gargantuan seatmate, who required two seatbelt extenders, was at least polite. He apologized every time he burped. All the evidence pointed to garlic salami.

This had to be considered cruel and unusual.

They should use this as an interrogation technique at Guantanamo Bay.

"Yes! I'll tell you where bin Laden is! Just don't belch on me anymore!"

I managed to wriggle one arm free and grabbed an air sickness bag, just in case.

Just as I thought the flight could get no worse the two kids in the seats directly in front of me began their act. Ramming the seat back onto my knees. Slamming their window screen up and down every thirty seconds. Screaming at each other. All to the apparent oblivion of their mother.

Fifty minutes after takeoff a flight attendant managed to get my attention.

"Is there anything you need sir?"

"Yes please. I need you to lock those two aggravating nematodes in the bathroom for the rest of the flight and send their mother to parenting school. Then tell the lady on the outside of my row that a few dabs of the three dollar perfume will suffice, a gallon is too much. And provide Jumbo here with a couple of dozen breath mints. That's all I need".

Actually I didn't say any of that. I didn't say anything because I could barely breathe so I just smiled weakly.

That had been a week earlier. I was roused from my reflections of the flight from Hades by the sight of someone moving toward me.

Low and behold. It was the very same farsighted gorgeous Texas woman from the first flight.

Hope springs eternal.

"Hey Lord, it's me again. Remember last week?"

CALLING UP TURKEYS |

My nephew and I have had a running discussion about turkey hunting.

My position was, the big goofy birds can't be that hard to hunt if the Indians killed them with rocks or bows and arrows.

The settlers managed to bag plenty of them with the unreliable old blunderbusses that they shot.

My nephew assured me that it's not as easy as it seems.

He said that the old gobblers are very easily spooked by something so slight as blinking eyes.

I remained skeptical but, he'd actually been turkey hunting and I never had.

Our conversation turned to turkey calling which is apparently an art unto itself. He uses three devices to call up turkeys. He demonstrated the first two, both hand held, and the sounds seemed authentic, at least to my ears.

Then he showed me one that he held in his mouth. It was small and thin and I was sure it wouldn't work but he made sounds that even I believed would attract a big Tom.

He handed me one and asked me to try it. He told me to press it to the roof of my mouth and try to say "choke, choke" and that should produce the correct sound.

I declined to try it there in front of him and his parents. Some of my kin don't believe it but there is a limit as to how foolish I will allow myself to look.

I promised to take it home and practice and when I mastered it I would show him.

The next day as I was driving back home I reached for the turkey call and popped it in my mouth. I figured nobody could hear me so I was safe.

"Press it to the roof of your mouth and try to say choke, choke".

It came out more like " Glub, glub".

I tried again. " Croak, croak"

Once more. " Glub, glub, croak croak".

I found out that it's possible to be totally embarrassed even when you're alone.

I put it aside and didn't pick it up again for a few days. I decided to try again one afternoon. I sat in my living room and attempted, over and over, to sound like a turkey. My neighbor knocked on the door, stuck his head in and asked me if I was okay. I hid the call behind my back and assured him I was fine. Just a little sore throat. I was gargling.

For my next try I went into the bathroom and turned on the shower so as not to alarm any other neighbors.

Just as I was about to " Choke, choke" I hiccuped and nearly swallowed the cussed thing! Suddenly I was "choking, choking"! I could breath but it was very uncomfortable.

As I was formulating how I could explain what happened to the paramedics the call dislodged itself. When it did, it slid back to the roof of my mouth and settled right in. My relieved gasp produced a perfect turkey call!

I was so proud!

It took nearly gagging to get it right but I did it!

The following Saturday I was back at the homeplace and decided to try out my new found skill. I went to a place where I knew there were turkeys and found myself a spot.

No gun. No camouflage. Just me and the little device.

I sat very still and began to call. " Choke, choke. Choke, choke".

Nothing happened but I kept at it.

" Choke, choke".

After about an hour I heard rustling in the trees above me.
Above me?

I hadn't been told that this could happen. I thought turkeys came in on the ground. I remembered my nephew's advice and remained very still, but I could definitely hear wings flapping from the trees as more birds landed.

"Choke, choke".

I heard another one land directly over me. Finally, unable to resist, I eased my head up and peeked.

Buzzards.

Dozens of them. No doubt attracted to the sounds of something dying down below. My sounds.

"Glub, glub, croak, croak".

I tossed the turkey call toward one of the nasty black birds as I stood up to walk out of the woods.

"Eat that", I said, and wondered if anybody would believe this tale.

Apparently, turkeys have gotten smarter since the Mayflower days while the pilgrims, such as me, have gotten less so. I've decided that the only way I am ever going to bag a wild turkey is if one surrenders to me.

But if anybody ever needs to call up a buzzard, I'm the man for the job.

In the meantime I will stick with Butterballs from Bi-Lo.

THIRTY, TWENTY |

3020.

Three zero, two zero.

Thirty, twenty.

Just a number.

It could have many different meanings.

It designates a century that will begin over a millinium from now. I hope it will be the number that the NASDAQ hits sometime in the next few years. It might be close to the number of pounds I've lost and gained and lost again over time. But in reality it means something entirely different to me.

Three Oh Two Oh was my link to home.

For over forty years 3020 was Mama's phone number. The phone book said it was Daddy's but he always tried to avoid the phone so it was really hers. It's the only phone number that she ever had. Imagine that! The same number since the early 60's!

The phone appeared about the same time as the indoor plumbing, when we moved into a new house when I was twelve. Before then, if some emergency required a phone call, we relied on what few neighbors had phones.

It's hard to imagine now but back then very few country homes had telephones. When we finally moved into the twentieth century, we were assigned the number 3020 and joined a party line with several other families, mostly kinfolk. In a precursor to today's ringtones, each family had its own ring. Ours was one long ring. Grandma's was one long ring followed by one short. Another cousin's was three short rings. One thing was certain, anybody could listen in, and they did, however I'm sure that national security was never compromised.

When we were first given the number you could simply dial 4-3020 from anywhere in the county to reach us. Years later the whole prefix became necessary. Even later an area code was added when the conversing population grew. Eventually callers were required to dial all ten numbers.

Times and dialing methods changed but 3020 remained constant. I dialed the number a thousand times from college either from homesickness or to beg for replenishment of funds.

The first time I dialed the number after I moved Out West, I was standing at a pay phone talking to Mama, telling her how fine the weather was in Colorado when out of nowhere came a freezing rain and sleet. In June. Mama took the opportunity to remind me that I could move back home anytime.

3020 represents a myriad of conversations about the highs and lows of life. It received and sent news of new babies and new life but also word of too many deaths, some expected, some devastating. It saw hundreds of minutes of uncomfortable silence that all teenagers experience when talking to someone of the opposite sex with absolutely nothing clever to say but with no inclination to hang up. Important calls, mundane calls, most now forgotten but some that never will be.

One year I dialed 3020 to tell Mama and Daddy the joyous news that, finally, the last of their children was getting married. Many years later I called again with the heartbreaking news that the marriage was over, the hardest call I ever made.

But between those calls, and since, there were plenty of occasions for rejoicing. Births and birthdays, graduations, promotions, travel plans, any event that needed to be shared. Calls made just for the comfort certain voices gave.

One year Mama called on my birthday and, not catching me at home, made Daddy sing Happy Birthday with her into the phone mail. When I heard it I could hear the embarrassment in his voice but I loved it and saved it for as long as the phone company allowed. The next year he died. I'd give anything to dial 3020 and hear his voice again.

Mama doesn't live at 3020 anymore. My brothers and I recently noticed that the line was dead. I had spoken to my sister about shutting it off since Mama had moved and we all have cell phones. I assumed that she had stopped the service and I felt an odd sadness at the thought that 3020 was gone. After a jillion phone calls, it was gone. The stories that 3020 could tell!

As it turned out, the phone was not shut off but had just been knocked out by recent heavy rains, but, for practical reasons, we decided to end phone service to the homeplace. Mama and Daddy would have totally understood the decision. Why pay for something that's never used.

So, 3020 will fade into our family history like the henhouse and the pig parlor.

Gone like the clunky black rotary phone which bore it. A thing of the past. The phone company will reassign the number with no thought of it's significance to one family. That's just the way it works.

3020.

More than just a number.

MOST EARNEST PRAYER |

Prayer.

Simple word. Powerful meaning.

Everybody I know prays or claims to.

I know without a doubt that hundreds of prayers have been said on my behalf throughout my life.

Asked and answered.

My family prays about everything and everybody and I've seen the results many times.

I got to thinking recently about the most earnest, most sincere prayers that I have ever offered up and, though there have been many, one stands out in my mind.

In a former life I was a street cop working mostly nights in a city of one hundred and forty thousand people. I worked the late shift by choice because I enjoyed the variety of nutcases who ventured out every night under the cover of darkness. It made the job much more interesting.

Most folks have no idea what goes on in their quiet little neighborhoods after nightfall. I used to tell my civilian friends that I had probably chased somebody through their backyard at 2am while they slept soundly, hopefully caught the bad guy, arrested, booked and jailed him before they woke up.

It was a fun career and I tried to keep praying throughout each shift. Prayers for my safety and for that of my fellow officers.

The story of my most earnest prayer began rather routinely.

I was dispatched to an apartment complex that was occupied mostly by Asian immigrants from Viet Nam, Cambodia and Thailand. The complaint was of an elderly Vietnamese woman standing outside of her apartment yelling curses at the neighborhood children who were playing a game in the lighted courtyard.

When I rolled up I saw the woman and noted that she was approximately 80 years old, around 4 feet 10 inches tall, and weighed around 80 pounds. I radioed that I would not need a back up car and headed to where she was squatting down with her back against the brick building. She looked ancient but her voice was strong and every time she shouted out in her native tongue the curse reverberated for blocks.

I couldn't understand a word she was saying so I stopped by the playground to ask some of the kids if they spoke her language. They did. They told me that she was angry because they were making too much noise playing. When they refused to go inside she began shouting and "calling down curses" on them.

After speaking with the kids I sent them into their apartments and decided to try to get the woman to go into hers. I walked over to her and asked, in English, which unit she lived in. She responded with a blood curdling string of shrieks that I was sure were more curses, this time being called down on me.

I motioned for her to stand up but she refused to budge. I tried again, same result. Finally, I reached down and took her by the elbow to help her stand. She appeared very frail so I was particularly careful.

I miscalculated.

As soon as I touched her elbow she exploded. She sprung up at me like a wolverine and latched onto my neck and shoulders in a death grip! The force knocked me backward and we both fell to the grass. She was clawing, punching and gouging, not the least bit intimidated by my fully equipped six foot four, two hundred and plenty more frame.

Makes for quite a mental picture doesn't it?

That's when my most earnest prayer began. It went something

like this.

" Dear Lord. Please do not let anybody that I know, or who might recognize me, drive by here and see me wrestling in the dirt with a woman who is twice my age and a third my size. Cause Lord, at the moment she is kicking my butt and I don't think I could live with the humiliation. If I am to die here, so be it. But I implore you, don't allow any of my cop friends to witness this."

I was finally able to pin her down and handcuff her. I took her in. It was bad enough having to walk into headquarters with my diminutive octogenarian arrestee, covered from head to boots with grass and mud, but at least nobody saw the encounter except Him and I'm sure He had a good laugh over it.

I learned two things.

NEVER underestimate your "opponent". I failed to take into account that the old woman came from a region at war for hundreds of years. I was just another small battle to her.

The other thing I learned?

Prayer works.

Ocean Awakening |

I have a confession.

It's difficult to talk about, embarrassing really, but I've learned that it's okay to bring it up occasionally. Battling any affliction requires being man enough to admit that it was once a part of you.

So, here goes.

I was once a confirmed, unapologetic, compulsive beach hater. There. Now you know.

That's a huge admission for a Southern boy who came of age with Jimmy Buffett and Bob Marley. Who was born and raised within a couple of hours drive of some of the best coastline in America.

However, at this juncture of my life, and once again living a stone's throw from the Atlantic and the Gulf of Mexico, I am no longer encumbered with the guilt that accompanied my desire to spend most of my summer days anywhere other than the seashore.

No more shame. I've seen the tide.

Garth Brooks got it right.

"I'm telling you, science has proved, that heartaches are healed by the sea."

I was re-enlightened again last week laying on the kind of beach I like. " After the season". No crowds. Not too hot. No boom boxes blaring out rap when everybody knows that the only acceptable beach music is, well, anything but rap.

It was nearly perfect. Except for the sand. I still don't like sand.

In the past I never looked toward the ocean for my respites. I've always been a mountain man not a beach boy.

I never particularly relished taking off my shirt in front of half a jillion people and trying to suck in my belly for the six hours I laid there sweating and sweltering.

And did I mention I don't like the sand?

I never understood what people found so marvelous about it.

Still, for several years I took my kids and joined the kin and friends for a few days at some beach or another. I played the good sport but they all knew I didn't enjoy the time the way they all seemed to.

Until one summer day on a sugar white strip of Carolina coastline.

That's when it happened.

I'd finally discovered a beach chair that was both comfortable and not terrifyingly flimsy. A balmy breeze was blowing. The noseeums were no shows. I was enjoying my favorite boat drink, minus the little decorative umbrella. I was surrounded by my family. I could hear the surf booming even with the beach music wafting through the Discman.

"I wanna go back, to the islands. Where the shrimp boats tie up to the pilings."

Epiphany!

I got it!

After all the years, I finally understood. I snatched off the headphones and shouted for joy!

"I never want to leave here!"

My fellow travelers gathered around me and broke into applause. Some had joyful tears in their eyes. Each one gave me knowing looks, as if I'd just graduated from a twelve step program.

Now I could be like them.

A beach person.

All proffered advice or encouragement.

Think melanoma, think sunscreen.

Tanned bellies are more attractive than white ones.

Always pick a spot close to a sunbather who resembles Free

Willy. You'll feel better about taking off the shirt.

The correct sunglasses allow unfettered and undetected bikini ogling.

Last week I sat on the beach thinking back on that new beginning. I crumbled up a handful of chips and tossed them toward a gang consisting of a hundred gulls, seven pigeons and one unidentified, deranged black featherball. Their chaotic choreography as they dashed for the barbecue flavored bits, all apparently Southern birds, was as entertaining as Riverdance.

Swimming in the warm saltwater eased the allover soreness caused by twenty years of street combat, and the sun, partially blockaded by the sunscreen, did indeed turn the old hide into a nicer shade of pale.

Contentment.

I have to admit, even after my enlightenment, that I still sneak off to my beloved mountains every now and then. But don't judge me because I am also happy to report that I have spent time on some beach, somewhere, every year since.

I'm cured.

I have a friend who goes into mourning on the day of the Autumnal Equinox, the technical end of Summer. She puts on sackcloth and ashes and there is much anguish and gnashing of teeth.

I try to soothe her as best I can. After all, it's just another date on the calendar. Down South, the weather stays nice enough for some sand and surf time till Halloween, and, you can arrive at some of the best coastlines in America before your second Kenny Chesney cd plays through.

Maybe I'll see you there over Labor Day. I'll be the one singing along with Brother Jimmy, "Mother, Mother ocean, I have heard you call..." and enjoying life on the beach.

Except for the sand. I still don't care for the sand.

See you at high tide.

SLIGHTLY OFF COURSE |

Have you ever been lost?

If you're a woman reading this, you probably have no trouble admitting that you've been lost.

Now, just the men.

Have you ever, in your entire life, even once, been lost?

Me either.

Daniel Boone, the great American frontiersman, once said " I've never been lost but I have been a mite bewildered for a week or two."

Old Daniel wandered around the wilds of Tennessee and Kentucky his whole life, before there roads, roadmaps or GPS devices. I can understand how he might have come to find himself in a situation where he didn't know exactly where he was. In the mountains all the ridges and streams and peaks can start to look alike.

I've been confused a couple of times on my solo hikes through the Rockies so I can sympathize with the old trailblazer.

But he and I have something else in common. A trait that we share with ninety-five percent of the male gender.

We never admit that we're lost.

Just a mite bewildered.

In Britain there is a quaint little thing called the roundabout. The stated purpose of the English roundabout, known in America as a traffic circle, is to maintain the safe, steady flow of vehicle passage through an intersection from all four directions at once.

In my reticent estimation, roundabouts and traffic circles are the worst ideas since the deep fried Twinkie. They require an unwary driver to make a split second decision which direction to go.

Driving through Salisbury, England, I actually drove through the very same roundabout from every different bearing and entered it from the North twice before I finally found my way out of town.

I involuntarily toured the city for two hours but I was never lost.

Simply somewhat baffled.

Another time I became rather puzzled in the Big Apple.

Being lost in New York City, not saying that I WAS lost, means hundreds of seemingly identical narrow streets, horrible traffic night and day, and very few friendly faces to ask directions of, even if you would stoop to such unmanly behavior.

I got so turned around that I began to imagine God turning to the One sitting at His right hand saying " Have you seen that Lively boy lately? I seem to have lost track of him."

"No Father, I haven't seen him since he crossed the Brooklyn Bridge."

You're pretty astray when the Lord can't find you.

The first summer I lived Out West I decided to spend a Saturday hiking. It was late August but I'd learned never to go anywhere in Colorado without a waterproof jacket, so I was armed with everything I needed for the day. That afternoon it began to cloud up so I expected it to rain awhile and clear up.

No rain.

Snow. In August.

Ok, technically it was sleet but it was still frozen water falling from the sky.

I was near timberline so I got under what passes for a tree that high up, more like a tangled thicket of bushes, to wait it out. When the sky cleared and I looked around I saw that the trail had vanished under the white blanket.

Not only was I instantly disoriented, I became just a tad concerned.

But not lost.

It was getting late and I knew better than to try to find my way out after dark. Going downhill in those mountains doesn't necessarily get you back to where you started. So I retreated back into my little den and spent my first night alone in the Rockies.

I passed the hours listening to a mountain stream somewhere in the distance roaring it's way down toward the plains. That was the first time I ever heard elk bugling. I saw stars so dazzling and so countless that I didn't want to sleep but the coyotes finally sent me there with their mournful lullabies.

The concern had disappeared. I was far from lost.

I was in Heaven on Earth.

I woke up to a late summer sun that had already melted away the sleet and there, right where I left it, was the trail.

That was one time when being a bit directionally befuddled turned out to be just fine with me.

Lost is just a state of mind and sometimes it's not such a bad thing.

I think Daniel Boone probably knew that since he purposely spent months at a time alone in the wilderness. He lived to be well over eighty years old and died peacefully on his front porch of natural causes.

Not the least bit bewildered.

THE BURNING TRUTH |

There's something about sitting around a fire with people you love that brings out the best, the most side splittingly funny, embarrassing, partly true partly fiction stories that get better every time they are re-told.

Fire away.

Southern folk, like us, you and me, love sitting around a campfire. Or a bonfire. Or just a pile of trash. We don't care. We'll light it up and watch it blaze.

We've even been known to burn old tires on a creek bank late at night.

Ever since some ancient man happened to be standing there when the first spark burst forth, fire therapy has healed more broken hearts, mended more spats and perpetuated more tales that eventually became accepted as factual family folklore than can possibly be numbered.

Fire therapy.

For the purposes I intend, I coined the phrase myself.

I know. If you Google "fire therapy" you'll find a few entries but they have nothing to do with what I'm talking about.

My version simply refers to the comfort given off by the combination of glowing embers, golden flames and revitalizing wood smoke.

When we think of the invention of fire we usually envision

some animal skin clad caveman striking two rocks together until the friction sparks ignited a dry leaf, thus, fire.

I don't really think that's what happened.

How on earth would men who had never seen fire before have any idea how to create one?

More likely, God looked down, obviously after Adam and Eve had been banished from Eden, and thought "These silly ones are going to freeze to death unless I help them."

He probably then sent down a bolt of lightening directly into a fat lighter stump.

Shazam!

Fire!

The old Texas trail bosses counseled young cowhands new to cattle driving to never sit and stare into a fire. The thought was, the bright flames affect your vision so if you are suddenly attacked by grizzlies or cougars, savage Indians or wild eyed Republicans, you couldn't see to defend yourself. Better to sit with your back to the flames. Get the benefit of the warmth while your eyes stayed focused on the darkness.

I'm sure that theory worked well for Charlie Goodnight's tired and dusty saddle bums but these days there's nothing as calming to weary souls as gazing into a good fire surrounded by kith and kin.

Add together a few hot dogs roasting or marshmallows browning over the coals, a competent firetender, and a few able storytellers to keep things lively, pun intended, and watch the wellness appear.

I'm confident that my prescription, used widely and often, could greatly diminish Prozac sales and render Dr. Phil unemployed.

On a recent chilly Saturday night cousins invited the local kinsmen to "come and set a while" around their firepit. Being inexplicably without a hot date, or even a lukewarm prospect for that matter, I decided to drop by.

The stories began to fly, some having been told hundreds of times but still worth a new turn.

Little brother Willie spun some pretty good yarns often using me as his dimwitted protagonist. I didn't really mind because the damnable lies, uh, the stories he told, I have to admit, were utterly entertaining. Of course I have my own stories on him, the difference being his humiliation just might find it's way into these pages one day.

Fireside gatherings are equal opportunity endeavors. Everybody gets a chance to be corrected, interrupted of talked over.

All in good fun.

The fire brings it out.

The group that night ran the gamut from the oldest, our host who by virtue of it being his place, was the tender of the fire, to the youngest, a sweet cousin who is waiting for her husband to return from the Middle East where he's serving bravely. She maintained a bemused look on her face that seemed to read " Could I really have sprung from the same seed as these lunatics?"

Get used to it Darlin. Some things even a good fire won't heal.

There's really only one hard and fast rule about fire sitting.

Poke it with a stick, adjust a log with your boot, add wood without permission from the firetender or in any other way molest the fire and ownership transfers to you and you have to take care of the fire till the next person makes the same mistake you did.

Never touch another man's fire.

One more thing.

If you brag that you can jump over the fire, be relatively certain that you can. "Almost" making it over the fire means you only "almost" avoided scorching your Levis.

But that's another story for another time.

Stay warm yall.

THE GAME |

Football.

It's just a game. Right?

Just a sports contest where opposing teams line up on opposite sides of the ball and see who can score the most points. All it really requires at the high school level is marginal speed and strength. There's really not much to be learned from twenty-two young men sweating, grunting and colliding for forty-eight minutes until one comes out the winner.

It's just a game. Correct?

Let me express a hale and hardy response to that assertion.

B.S.

Thank you.

Now allow me to bust that myth wide open.

All it really requires to know that it's much more than " just a game ", at least to the players and coaches, is to look into their eyes after they have laid it all on the line for ten or twelve weeks, spent countless hours practicing, learning, improving, then played and coached their guts and hearts out but still came up just a bit short of their ultimate goal.

At a recent post-game gathering, the last one for this year, those eyes betrayed an array of emotions.

Shock. Anger. Disbelief. Sadness. Heartache.

Why?

Why does this silly little game inspire such wrenching feelings? Because it's more than just a game.

More than any other game football requires teamwork. Every player has an assignment on every play. Some positions shine more brightly than others but every position is important. Whether you're rich or poor, from the country or from town, on the field you're just one part of a system that by design needs all the other parts.

Sounds a little bit like life doesn't it?

You have to prepare for this game. Practice till you're sick to death of practice, then practice some more. That's how you get better than the other teams, how you win more than you lose.

Be better than the other guy and success is guaranteed.

That's a life lesson.

Here's another, one that I wish every coach in America would pound in from day one of the summer sessions.

Enjoy this time.

Enjoy the game.

If it's not fun, don't play.

Enjoy the game so much that you can't wait for Friday nights to roll around. Can't wait to deliver that first smackdown. Can't wait to hear the crowd, your crowd, roar for you.

Enjoy the smell of the turf and the feel of the black greasepaint under your eyes.

Enjoy it so much that when the realization strikes that it's over, really over, and when you take off those smelly old shoulder pads some night that it will be for the final time, something happens that you're not accustomed to, not prepared for, being the rough and rowdy that you are.

You cry.

Impossible.

Big boys don't cry.

While we're destroying fabrications let me take a shot at that one.

Big boys don't cry?

Trust me. They do. Big, strong, strapping, fire snorting, ornery boys do cry.

And why not.

The field where I stood as one of the crowd recently held more wet eyes than dry ones. Not just the players either.

Parents. Friends. Fans. Girlfriends.

And big boys.

Some just wanted to be left alone. No amount of " it was a great season" or "just wait till next year" could console, particularly not the seniors. Those words will ring hollow and taste bitter until some time has passed. But on the other side of that emotion were the kin and friends who knew nothing else to do but comfort, or at least try. Mamas and Daddies wanted to hug their boys and try to find the one thing they could say that would magically make it okay again.

It wasn't going to happen.

Because amidst all the tears and anger and shock one fact remained that was never spoken aloud.

They're just kids.

These tough talking, hard charging well coached and well trained athletes, these big boys who shouldn't cry, are kids.

Of course I know that not one of them would admit that. In their own minds they are men, able and ready.

I understand that part too, but the fact is, the two descriptions don't necessarily contradict.

The Daddies understand that. So do the Mamas.

One day, when other football seasons have come and gone, all of those tough guy players will understand too.

Because, while football is not war and not rocket science, the lessons learned from this game we Southerners love can take the participants far in another game we also love, the game of life.

One of those lessons is very simple.

Big boys do indeed cry.

And that's just fine.

Because it's more than just a game.

Rainfall And Roundups |

Nearly every year the Blessed South is blessed with a drought that can last anywhere from a few weeks to several months.

And every year the folks around these parts do what they've been doing since the first Scot-Irish settlers arrived.

Pray for rain.

One year the dry spell became so dire that the governor led a prayer session on the steps of the state capitol. Churches from all of the affected areas held special services for the sole purpose of praying for much needed moisture. I attended assemblies at several different congregations and the entreaty was always the same.

"Lord, we need rain. "

There were plenty of cynical scoffers. The governor was ridiculed by some. So was anybody who believed that prayer could break a drought. Some editorialists even railed against the use of state time and expense for such measures.

But then something happened.

It rained.

It rained a lot in some areas, less in others, but the water did arrive. Around our place water stood in the low spots for weeks.

I wasn't surprised.

I know why it rained.

Daddy taught me years ago.

We stood on the edge of a field watching the first irrigation system he ever installed shooting thousands of gallons of water onto the parched crops. I had never seen such a rig and was amazed.

"Daddy, this thing is great! It'll cover this whole field in a couple of days". I marveled.

He just continued to look out over the field.

"Son, the Good Lord can do the same thing in fifteen minutes", he said, then added rather cynically, " I just wish He WOULD".

He explained that the irrigation system was just a stop gap measure until the rains came. He said, "The Good Lord (I never heard Daddy refer to God by any other name except The Good Lord) knows when it needs to rain and He'll send it when He decides to".

Daddy might have been a little impatient, but he knew who was really in charge.

Years later and many miles from the farm, I was with a friend in the Chuchara Valley in southern Colorado. She worked part time on a ranch owned by an old gentleman whose family had moved Out West from Alabama after the Civil War ended. The ranch was nestled between rolling foothills to the east and the Sangre de Cristo mountains to the west.

I struck up a great friendship with the rancher and one year I asked him to let me help with his Fall roundup. I assured him that I could ride. That was true.   I also convinced him that I could rope. That was a ball faced lie but I figured I could fake it for a while and learn on the run, literally. During the week I did manage to get a rope on a few steers and, in doing so, provided the real cowhands with enough entertainment that they wouldn't let the owner run me off when he realized that I had deceived him about my ability with a lariat.

Actually, he may have had an inkling that I had fudged the facts a bit because he assigned me a horse that I'm sure was spawned by Satan himself. But the animal and I came to an understanding after an hour or so the first day, and were quite a team by the end of the roundup. Roping steers is hard enough on the flats but much trickier in a fir thicket in the Rockies.

On my last day I sat in the saddle with the owner and my friend, also still mounted, atop a rise overlooking his ranch. From there we could see the whole valley before us. Beyond the valley the sun was beginning to disappear behind the white peaks. We saw hundreds of cows dotting the valley floor. I was in awe.

"You have it made here," I said. " I'd give anything to have a tenth of what you have".

The old man just held his gaze on the vista below. He pondered a moment, then asked, " Partner, do you know David?"

Speaking before thinking, as usual, I asked " David who, sir?"

He laughed. " I'm referring to the Psalmist, in the Bible".

"Oh, well sure", I replied, not wanting to appear any more simpleminded than I already did.

"Well David made it clear that God owns the cattle on a thousand hills. Everything you see down there belongs to Him. I'm just the caretaker". He chuckled, " Even those two that it took you all week to rope are His ."

"Three!" I corrected him as we headed the horses downhill.

While we rode I had a déjà vu moment and remembered Daddy all those years before explaining how the rain came when God let it.

Others can doubt and scoff. As for me, I'll rely on the wisdom of one old farmer and one old rancher.

And the Good Lord.

Batchin' It |

I thought I'd broken my toe and cut loose with a string of words, none of which you will ever hear in a Sunday sermon. I realized, too late, that there was a lady behind me pushing a grocery cart. I had to apologize to her for my bad, albeit totally understandable, language.

It hurt.

How, you might ask, does one break a toe in a supermarket?

It's not all that difficult.

Just allow a sixteen ounce can of collard greens to fall out of your cart and land on your sandal clad foot.

The lady was kind. She accepted my contrition then reached into my cart to adjust the little flap that covers the hole on the back end, thereby preventing any further errant food items from escaping and doing me further injury.

Who knew there was a flap?

This is why God made women. To save men from themselves.

In the first two chapters of Genesis, when God was creating things and putting the universe in order, He was pretty happy with His work.

He created light and darkness, night and day, and, " He saw that it was good."

He created the earth and the water and the sky, and, " He saw that it was good."

Vegetation. Seeds. Fruit trees. "Good."
Sea life. Birds. Livestock. Wildlife. Crawling creatures.
Etcetera, etc. All good.
Till He made a single man.
Not so good.
"It is not good for the man to be alone"
He realized right away that throughout human history men would need women to maintain harmony.

I agree with that scripture and not just because it's a sin to disagree.

Having lived alone for the past several years I rely on a bevy of women friends to help me negotiate life's twists and turns. My sister, my daughters, a few cousins, and one former girlfriend with whom I parted ways but who was amused enough by my misadventures that she still hangs around.

I told some of them the canned goods injury story. Two of them laughed so hard they were not able to give me any advice. Another simply rolled her eyes and muttered something about my breeding.

One gaped at me.

"Why in Heavens name would you buy collard greens in the can instead of fresh or at the very least frozen. Canned?"

She was dumbfounded and missed the whole point of the story.

"I'm sorry. Living away from the South all those years perverted my culinary intelligence."

Recently I came across a small pillow that my grandmother made me for Christmas many years ago. It's several decades old and had gotten stained so I put it in the washer with a load of towels. Just after the wash cycle began I opened the lid to put in one more thing. There, churning on top of the water, were millions of tiny pieces of orange foam rubber.

I took that to be a clue that something had gone wrong.

So that's what Grandma stuffed the pillow with.

It was destroyed.

I told one of my lady kinfolk about it.

"You should have tied it up in a big pillowcase and washed it that way," she said, and added, " or just washed it by hand."

"I wish you'd told me that sooner," I sighed.

"Well, I wouldn't expect even you to throw a family heirloom into your Maytag."

For the record, it was a Kenmore and it wasn't mine, it was Mama's.

I didn't even bother to seek female assistance when I needed to alter a clothing item that I was coerced into wearing for a special event. I needed to resize the item and, since the altered part wouldn't be visible, I used duct tape. It worked and nobody knew except for a couple of friends with whom I entrusted the information.

One of those "friends" promptly described my tailoring method to our Sunday School class. Some of the women in the room wept tears of pity for me.

Hey, I never claimed to be Calvin Klein.

If I ever have another mishap in the grocery store you can be certain that when I tell the story it will be a can of something much more normal to Southern cuisine and thereby more likely to draw sympathy from my female think tank.

Perhaps boiled peanuts.

And as for that antique pillow that Grandma made for me, it was pretty much a total loss. I have no idea how to repair it except for one possibility.

"In 1942 man invented duct tape and saw that it was good."

Amen.

The Ride |

In another life I was a street cop for over twenty years.

It wasn't always fun, but it was never boring.

One night I was dispatched to a domestic dispute between a man and his wife. He'd broken her nose so I took an immediate dislike to him. He was also drunk and very angry and had no intention of going to jail, so he fought.

He was about my size but younger so it took me a few minutes to get him in custody. With assistance from a couple of other officers I strapped him into the back of my patrol car even though he was still kicking and screaming and calling me names that weren't even in the proverbial book yet.

Fighting gets the adrenaline pumping for the good guys and the bad guys so as I got into the front seat of the car I was still hyped up, sweating buckets, and a little bit winded. I had a torn shirt and could taste my own blood in my mouth.

And I was Southern boy mad.

It was one of those times when I fantasized about taking the punk down some dark road and administering a little country justice. Every ounce of my being wanted to continue the fight and show this guy that I would not be assaulted and abused by him, nor would I allow him to beat up his wife without some serious consequences. It was not my religion that kept me from seeking vengeance, at least I didn't think so at that moment. I was more concerned about the legal repercussions of such impetuous measures.

I managed to get myself under control, but the thoughts I was having were very Un-Christian, to put it mildly.

I wiped the blood from my lip and radioed headquarters that I would be enroute to the jail with a male prisoner, "uncooperative and combative". That would alert the jail personnel to be ready for a fighter. Then I began the twenty minute drive to lock-up, otherwise know as the Graystone Hotel. As I drove, my detainee in the back seat continued to kick and shout and cuss at me and I allowed myself to feel disgust, and almost real hatred, toward him.

Then something happened that I will never forget.

Five minutes into the trip the man suddenly stopped yelling and got very quiet. I thought that he might have passed out but I was so thankful for the silence that I didn't even check him. Then I heard him say something.

" Officer, sir?"

Suddenly I'd gone from being a fat bleeping bleep to Officer Sir. Something was obviously wrong.

I finally asked him what he wanted.

" Can you please turn that up?" he asked.

I still wasn't sure what he meant so I asked him again.

" Please turn up the radio."

I understood then, and I was stunned.

Earlier in the shift I'd been listening to a Christian station but I had turned the volume down when I drove up to the scene of the dispute. I could barely hear it but he could, through the back speakers. I turned it up and heard one of the beautiful songs of praise that the station plays all night. I heard it, but more importantly, the broken man in the back seat heard it too.

When the song finished another began, even more meaningful to the moment than the first one.

" In my darkest hours He will guide me, and I will not be afraid, no I will not be afraid."

A few minutes later I heard the man, the same one who had not long before split my lip, weeping quietly as we drove, then louder until he was sobbing from somewhere deep in his heart.

While I'd been building up a healthy hate for him, God had been touching his life through the words and melodies of the nameless singers inside the radio.

I was quickly thrown into quite a state of confusion.

I was still mad. I didn't particularly want to share my Lord with the same man who had shown such a blatant disregard for the health of his wife, and for mine.

Fortunately for humanity, God never asks my opinion.

When I turned the man over to the deputies he looked at me and said " I'm sorry, sir."

Just " I'm sorry" , but so heartfelt.

I didn't always listen to the Christian station that was tuned in, but that night I was.

Cynics might call it coincidence.

Not me. I call it intervention.

Not always fun. Never boring.

" Blessed are the peacemakers for they shall be called the sons of God."

Snake Tales |

" I'd rather fight a grizzly bear than a snake", I once told a Colorado buddy.

"That 's cause you've never met up with a grizzly in the wild", he replied.

He was right, but I'd still prefer the bear. At least you see the bear coming. Just clamber up a tall tree and hope that he's already eaten somebody else and isn't hungry.

Or hope that you've been fortunate enough to stumble onto a vegetarian bear.

Regardless of the bear's dietary preferences, I'll take my chances.

Of all God's creations the only one I fear is snakes.

Any snake. Any kind. Any size.

I have a rational explanation for this irrational fear.

You never see the snake until it's right under your foot.

When that happens to me one of two things occur.

I get bit or I have a mini coronary and since I have never actually been bitten it might help to explain my recent heart trouble. It makes perfect sense now that I think about it. I've had many close encounters with the slithering devils none of which was pleasant and most of which caused my ticker to skip a few ticks.

Snakes are evil.

When I was a kid my big brother Urb and I were picking blackberries in the woods. The patch was really thick and we were out in the middle of it eating about as much of the sweet fruit as we were loading into the pans that Mama had provided. Without warning a huge coachwhip poked his head straight up out of the bushes as if it was standing on it's tail and came face to face with us. I flashed back to every film clip I'd ever seen about cobras, had the first of many imaginary heart attacks, and tore out of that berry field a lot less carefully than I had gone in, ripping my bare legs from knees to ankles. Urb was right behind me laughing all the way.

I wasn't amused.

Years later I was informed by a supposed reptile expert that snakes can only raise a third of their total length off the ground. If that's true then my berry patch snake had to measure fifteen feet or more.

One day I was fishing in the sloughs near the river. The place was choked with weeds and as I was crossing the branch I felt something bump against my boot. I looked down just in time to see a small brown colored snake make a second strike toward my ankle. I didn't wait around for a third attempt, jumped straight up, walked on air somehow defying gravity, and landed six feet away.

I'm not normally that agile but that day Air Lively would have put Air Jordan to shame.

I later learned that my attacker was a hognose, the type that will strike without opening it's mouth apparently to scare it's opponent into retreating.

Mission accomplished.

Another time I was fishing, this time in a john boat in Brier Creek, with a man that worked with us on the farm. He was even more afraid of snakes than I was and he carried a pistol to dispatch any that he saw.

As we floated down the creek we bumped against an overhanging limb causing a sunning snake to fall into the boat directly between my friend and me. Saying that he panicked would understate it. It was more like hysteria. He snatched the revolver out of his pocket and fired all six rounds at the snake.

And shot six holes in the bottom of the wooden boat.

Never touched the snake.

It only took the boat a few minutes to sink causing all three occupants, the snake included, to swim for shore.

I was actually laughing too hard to be scared that time but as a result I swallowed a few gallons of creek water.

We never did recover the boat.

No doubt, having snakes for neighbors is part of living in the South. Rattlers. Moccasins. Corals down in Florida.

All deadly. All villainous.

I know some people who actually like snakes and don't share my belief that they are Satan incarnate but I tend to agree with Daddy who used to paraphrase Genesis, the Bible book, not the 80's rock group, on the subject of snakes.

" Bruise his (the serpent's) head lest he bruise thy heel", he'd say.

I concur.

After all, there are reasons why God condemned snakes to crawl on their bellies and eat dust their whole lives.

Because they're wicked.

And they cause heart trouble.

Hitting The Trail |

Recently, a friend invited me to come ride horses on his little farm.

"It's been ten years since I sat a horse," I replied, thinking back on the hundreds of trail miles I rode through the Rocky Mountains, every foot of it an adventure.

"Well, it's just like riding a bicycle. You never forget how." He was grinning when I turned to face him.

"Yea, right," I grinned back.

We both knew better.

All bikes operate pretty much the same. You straddle it. You peddle it. Maybe you shift gears every now and then. It's pretty much the same as it was all those years ago when your Daddy promised you he wouldn't let go when he was pushing you on your first little Schwinn.

Daddy lied.

He let go. You crashed. You cried. But eventually you learned to ride a bike.

And you probably never forgot how.

Horses are different.

Horses don't come equipped with training wheels.

No two horses are alike in temperament. Trust me on that. But I have a theory that all horses do share one common trait.

More about that later.

Everybody loves horses, right?

Depending on your point of view, horses can be regal and proud, frisky and cute, or swift and powerful.

If you've been around a few decades you instantly recognize the names of certain horses such as Roy Roger's faithful steed, Trigger.

You may have read Black Beauty or seen the movie based on the classic children's novel.

Horses were a part of growing up.

My friend Flicka.

Mister Ed.

Hi ho Silver, away!

Dusty.

Dusty?

You may not have heard of Dusty.

He was mine. Well, partly mine. I had a one fourth interest in him, having to share him with my three sibs.

Dusty only got in a hurry when he headed toward his oat bin. One day Urb and I, and another kid were all astride the old boy when he lit out for the barn. We couldn't rein him down and when he ran under the barn door we were toppled off his back like dominoes.

Once I was loping across a mountain meadow aboard Old Major, my favorite horse of all time. My hat blew off and when I stopped to retrieve it the rest of the group kept riding. Every time I tried to re-mount, Major began his little sideways crow-hop dance. By the time he and I came to a mutual understanding, and I was back on him, my friends were two canyons ahead.

Another time I was riding a horse aptly named Diablo, which means Devil south of the Rio Grande. We were getting along fine till he intentionally ran under a telephone pole guy-wire and cleaned me off the saddle as slick as a whistle.

Then there was Taffy, my cousin EJ's palomino. I had him loping down a firebreak behind Grandma's house one Sunday afternoon when we came to a fork in the path. I wanted to go right. Taffy decided to go left. We parted company and I ended up in a barbwire fence.

Taffy got back to the barn before I did.

See, all horses do have one thing in common.

They don't want you, or me, or anybody else on their back.

I don't care how sweet and gentle your animal is. It doesn't matter how gently he nibbles that sugar cube off your palm, or how he lovingly runs to the gate every time you approach the corral.

He does not want to be ridden.

It's just a plain fact if you ride horses long enough, sooner or later, you'll wake up on your back in the mud wondering where your horse disappeared to and why there are little birds flying around in your head.

But despite my own few mishaps, I do still love the cussed beasts. Old Major in particular. He could be ornery but he was also tall and strong.

And surefooted.

He rode me across the Continental Divide by way of some treacherous trails that I'd have never thought we'd survive, my inside leg scraping a sheer rock wall, outside leg hanging over a thousand foot cliff.

It was terrifyingly exhilarating.

Some of the most beautiful sights I ever saw Out West were seen from horseback.

I admit it. I'm a saddlebum wannabe.

My favorite literary philosopher, Augustus McCrae, of the sweeping western novel Lonesome Dove, said it best:

"I can't think of nothing better than riding a fine horse into a new country."

I couldn't agree more, and I look forward to taking my friend up on his offer to ride.

But I'll be keeping a tight rein just in case the horse is in agreement with my theory.

Happy trails.